R0103531881

DENMARK

1 COPENHAGEN. Gammel Strand (the Old Quay) in the centre of the City. The baroque spire of St. Nicolai is in the background

DENMARK

By
Sacheverell Sitwell

London
B. T. BATSFORD LTD

First published 1956

PRINTED AND BOUND IN GREAT BRITAIN BY
WILLIAM CLOWES AND SONS, LIMITED, LONDON AND BECCLES
FOR THE PUBLISHERS
B. T. BATSFORD LTD.
4, FITZHARDINGE STREET, PORTMAN SQUARE
LONDON, W.1

To
CLAUS AHLEFELDT

PREFACE

THIS book is dedicated to my friend Claus Ahlefeldt, at whose instigation I went to Denmark in August 1954. H. E. the Danish Ambassador in London, Mr. Steensen-Leth, kindly encouraged the project by giving me letters, more particularly to Mr. Sigurd Christensen, the Chef du Protocol of the Danish Foreign Office, who did everything in his power to assist and facilitate my enquiries, not least by handing me over eventually to his assistant Mr. N. A. Holck-Colding, who, with his brother the expert on miniature painting, has procured most of the illustrations for this book.

It is owing to the help and patience of others that this volume has been able to appear at all in its present form. Through the kind services of Mr. Christensen I was introduced to Mr. Boesen, Inspector of the Rosenborg Collection, who enabled me to see many of the Rosenborg treasures in private, not least the rare and beautiful Persian 'polonaise' carpets which are part of the Coronation regalia. To Mr. Christensen I owe, also, an introduction to Mr. Bjørn Rubov of the State Museum of Art; and enquiries which were made on my behalf from Mr. Bjørn Kornerup, Ph.D., Historian of the Royal Danish Orders, and Mr. Arne Hoff, Inspector of the Arsenal Museum, both of whom did their best to answer questions about the history and origin of the heyducks' uniforms. A special, and I believe unique photograph of one of the heyducks in his 'flower-pot' hat was taken by the Court Photographer. Letters of introduction to Miss de Bardenfleth, Prioress of Vemmetofte, and to Countess Moltke, Deaconess of Vallø, came from the same source; and Mr. Christensen, as well, obtained permission from Count Holstein to visit his castle of Ledreborg, put me in touch with the owner of Clausholm, and tried to arrange for me to see the 'Grauballe man' at the Pre-Historic Museum at Aarhus. It is evident from all this that I owe a debt of thanks and gratitude to Mr. Sigurd Christensen, and I would like, also, to thank him and his English wife, the writer Monica Redlich, for hospitality in their delightful home. I must also thank Mr. Harald Langberg for the loan of photographs of stucco details from Frederiksberg, my regret being that I have as yet had no opportunity of seeing his lately published book on the buildings and stucco work of Denmark.

It is a pleasant task to add a special note of thanks to Danish friends. The dedication of this book will show my gratitude to Count Claus Ahlefeldt-Laurvig. Perhaps the clou or climax of a month in Denmark was staying at his mother's house at Gedser, which was my first and memorable experience of a Danish home. Another friend of longer standing, Countess Helle Danneskjold-Samsø, made several excursions with us, and in the guise of Prioress of Gisselfeld took us to luncheon at that nun-less nunnery with its corridors lined with china, its romantic lakes and tall old trees. I would also thank Mr. Robert Coe, U.S. Ambassador in Denmark, who has so many friends in England; and Stephen Fox-Strangways, on holiday from Eton, who took the photograph of Ledreborg.

Danish friends, whom we met for the first time, include Baron Reedtz-Thott, who showed us the huge portrait collection at Gaunø on our way to Falster. Through the particular kindness of the owner, Baron Juel-Brockdorff, we were enabled to see Valdemar Slot, one of the most beautiful of old Danish castles, with its portraits by Carl Gustav Pilo; while at Glorup, the property of Count Moltke-Huitfeldt, we saw this old house with its formal canal and clipped trees. Wedellsborg has perhaps a greater renown than any other house in Denmark. To its owner, and to Countess Wedell, I would express a special word of thanks. Another old house, Gyldensten, also in Funen, recalls particular memories because of the beautiful objects in it and what I would call its 'Danishness'.

In Jutland we stayed with Count Tido Wedell at his castle of Frijsenborg; were taken by him to luncheon at the delightful manor house at Tvede; and were introduced by him into the old and enchanted castle of the Rosenkrantzs, almost an unnerving experience for an Englishman. That this family whose name was on the lips of Shakespeare should still be living in their castle of Rosenholm is nearly too good to be true, and I could never forget their family tombs at Hornslet. Such an accumulation of the raw material of poetry is seldom seen. To Baron Berner-Schilden-Holsten I owe permission to see the interior of Clausholm, an old house for which I think I have sufficiently expressed my admiration in the pages that follow. And now I hope and believe I have thanked everyone in Denmark who was friendly and kindly to us, leaving till last the old lady, a rose-lover, or as I prefer it, *rosomane*, who got into touch with me over my abortive seeking for the Yellow Cabbage rose and asked me to stay with her in her thatched cottage on the isle of Fanø, late in August, while the roses were still in bloom. I do not recall her name. But, even now, this is not all my thanks. For I must mention Mme Vera Volkova, who helped to the perfection of Margot Fonteyn's dancing, who now teaches the Russian 'school' to the Royal Danish Ballet, and who took us to see her pupils in class. My thanks go, also, to Mr. Niels Bjørn Larsen, their Maître de Ballet. And lastly I must thank my wife, who drove me all over Denmark without once colliding with a bicycle, who, as ever, helped and encouraged me with my writing, and who read my proofs.

It is unfortunately true that it is never possible to see everything. I have for instance not yet seen a performance by the Royal Danish Ballet. I am aware, too, that in missing the island of Fanø, I have not seen something uniquely typical of Denmark. But I am sorrier, still, not to have gone to Tønder, that little town down near the German frontier which, I think, must be the prettiest place in the Kingdom. I am at least able to quote with permission from John and Phyllis Cradock *(Bon Viveur's)* charming account of it. I tried to visit as many as I could of the country houses but some few have still eluded me. Sophieholm, for example, described sometimes as the most beautiful house of the rococo period in Denmark; and Frederiksdahl which Mrs. Constance Villiers-Stuart in a recent article in *Country Life* (1 September 1955) describes with its family and Royal portraits, large flower paintings, and paintings of birds by Tobias Stranover, a Hungarian who also worked in England. Perhaps, these apart, and the interior of Fredensborg and the inside of the cathedral at Aarhus, I saw most of what there is to be seen in Denmark.

There is, in the Danes and in Denmark, so much that is in our common ancestry. For to certain parts of England the Danes were more important and have left a more lasting influence than either the Normans or the Saxons. I am thinking particularly of Lincolnshire and its vicinity. If Aalborg in Jutland is the place of eels, is not Selby in Yorkshire the 'seals' house' from the number of seals formerly taken there? Danish must have been commonly spoken in this district over several hundred years; though history is not so simple as that and the village names Frieston, Friskney, Firsby, all on or near the coast, are said to denote colonies from Friesland. So, in fact, Denmark is not like England in general, but only like a part of England and it no more resembles the rest of Great Britain than it is the counterpart to Norway or to Sweden. Yet a country district where it is possible to pick fifty current surnames out of a local telephone directory which are of Danish origin, including such names as Alger, Basker, Dring, Humble, Kettle, Odell, Swales and Tovey (*Lincolnshire and the Fens*, by M. W. Barley, p. 95, 1952) must show that we and the Danes have ties of blood as well as those links which attach Stratford-on-Avon to the ramparts and bastions of Elsinore. If so, it may be a consanguinity in both kinds which has made it that the only two Victoria Crosses ever awarded to non-Englishmen have been given to Danes.

Denmark occupies a small area, and on a map of the world is little more than an island or two and a point or extremity of land. Yet many persons of experience would put Copenhagen after Rome, Paris and London, as a pleasure capital of Europe with the equivalent of a perpetual summer fair or festival, the Tivoli Garden, open all day and every evening in its midst. And that is indeed one of the delights of the Danish capital. There is, or appears to be, no poverty, which is another of its attractions compared to Rome or Paris. The

12

Danes seem to have solved of instinct some of the more terrible and besetting problems of living in the modern world. Something peculiar to Danish towns is to see a whole kindergarten of small children attached by strings to their nurse or teacher, and crossing the road. Fair hair in children is as universal as dark, woolly curls upon the banks of Niger. Much in Denmark is as new and brightly painted as the ideal classroom in an infants' school. The landscape can be like a nursery wallpaper. But, in the same breath, the Danes love and preserve the old; and this is why Denmark is one of the most delightful and pleasing of all countries in Europe for a spring, summer, or autumn holiday. The middle one of which alternatives is my excuse and reason for this present book.

2 December 1955   *Sacheverell Sitwell.*

Postscript. As this Preface goes to press Mr. Holck-Colding informs me that the mystery has been solved as to the 'Crowned Empress' on the monument to Jørgen Scheel in Auning Church (see pp. 141, 142). He has consulted Dr. Thorlacius-Ussing's book on the sculptor Th. Quellinus. From this it appears that the lady is not Catherine the Great, but Jørgen Scheel's wife Benedicte Brockdorff who, 'with diamonds in her hair, and with ornaments and fine lace, proudly looks down from the epitaphium which she has erected to her late husband'.

CONTENTS

ACKNOWLEDGMENT

FIGURE 36 is reproduced by Gracious Permission of Her Majesty the Queen.

The Author and Publishers wish to thank the following for permission to reproduce the other illustrations appearing in this book:

The Chronological Collection of the Danish Kings at Rosenborg, for figs. 11 and 12; Elfelt, Copenhagen, for fig. 13; Stephen Fox-Strangways, for fig. 29; Eric de Maré, for figs. 1–3, 21 and 30; The National Historical Museum at Frederiksborg, for figs. 10, 19, 20, 23–5, 27 and 37; National Museum, Copenhagen, for figs. 4–6, 39 and 40; National Museum, Stockholm, for fig. 38; National Travel Association of Denmark, for fig. 33; Ny Carlsberg Glyptotek, for fig. 35; Paul Popper Ltd., for fig. 22; Royal Danish Ministry for Foreign Affairs, for figs. 15 and 42; The State Museum of Art, for figs. 26, 31 and 34; Stiftung Oskar Reinhart, for fig. 28; Swedish Travel Bureau, for fig. 32; Tilhøer Tivoli, for figs. 7–9; Messrs. Wartski, London, for fig. 14.

Their thanks are also due to the Royal Institute of British Architects for loaning their copy of "Den Danske Vitruvius" from which figs. 16–18 are reproduced.

LIST OF ILLUSTRATIONS

CHAPTER I

Across Denmark

HARWICH, port of embarkation for Esbjerg, is pervaded with a southern *dolce far niente* on the August Sunday afternoon. This seems, somehow, so inappropriate to British Railways. But groups of porters stood about doing nothing at all in the damp drizzle. And they were present in large numbers. Except for the fine rain, it was like a scene of old in a southern Italian railway station. Two or three porters to every passenger, but none of them interested. So it used to be, as, now, on Britain's East Coast. Previously, there had been maddening delays at level crossings. A single engine running backwards and forwards, light-heartedly, and much lingering over a local train before the boat-express came in. Then, a quick burst of energy, of southern fire, as though the platform gave on to Vesuvius and the Bay of Naples. What will be the end when this southern indolence has paralysed all nationalized industries in our wet climate? Even the police constable on duty at the level crossing said he had never known such laziness, that there were men standing and sitting about idle all day, doing nothing, and that someone should complain. But there at the embarkation platform was the long white ship, more like a private yacht; the cabins on board, small, but scrupulously clean, and the only difficulty the early hour of dinner, two hours even so, after lifting anchor; after steering out through the shoals into the sunset; watching the headlands straighten themselves out and fade back, one by one; and passing the hulk of a Norwegian oil-tanker, still burning and belching forth black smoke, with a smaller French boat attached to it and towing

19

it, rather as an insect will carry along a bigger insect. And as we watched this sinister-looking arrest and forced march upon the darkening waters, the other passengers were eating, and we came down to a late dinner at about eight o'clock.

Upon these Scandinavian boats it is almost impossible to tell the difference between first and second class. Walking on deck in the morning one could see the *smørrebrød* luncheon being laid out as one passed the windows of the dining saloons, and on each table the number of little dishes was nearly incredible, particularly in what seemed the nicer of the two, which turned out to be the cheaper class. The shipping company, most obviously, make it a point of propaganda to provide this amazing meal just before disembarkation, going either way. Its character can be indicated in a phrase when we say it would delight a pelican. Herring in various forms its chief component, but all served up to look as appetizing as possible, and every tin virgin and untouched. No such thing as a tin of herring from which someone else has helped himself; and we shall find that this is a principle throughout Denmark, as it is, indeed, in Sweden and in Norway, too. The *smørrebrød* gives, at once, a national character to what might otherwise have been a boring meal, though I could not help being reminded of the wartime experience of a friend who had been lecturing in Sweden. On his return he was given a delicious Swedish luncheon in the aeroplane, but on arrival over English waters the windows were sealed, so that you could not look out, and the same crew served him a traditionally nasty English dinner. Luncheon, to-day, was early; as early as dinner had been last night, which was at six-thirty.

But, now, we were just off Esbjerg, and everyone has to be off the boat at half-past twelve. It is of no use to pretend that the port or harbour is of absorbing interest. There are no old Hanseatic warehouses, as at Bergen in Norway, nor is it a fine new town, as Göteborg in Sweden. Our 'national newspapers' a week old in the shops, and an amber necklace or two from the sands of Fanø. Of which more later. But Esbjerg is just Esbjerg, the port of entry into Denmark. A place, however, where customs' formalities are reduced to the sensible minimum, and in a few moments you are back again in your car free to go where you will. We had planned to spend the first two nights at Odense, on the middle island, but distances are so small in Denmark and the roads so good that there was time to make a detour and go down south a little to the town of Ribe.

A gentle drizzle in Denmark, taking the form of 'light luncheon rain', beginning the moment we came into harbour, and perhaps in order to remind us that we were still opposite our native land. Nothing of interest at all in Esbjerg, excepting for persons absorbed in the words of the guide book in "fishing iceworks, cold stores, and fillet facts". A town built on "a patch of moor", where only twenty people were living in 1865, who must have been buffeted to bits by the winds and had sand constantly blown into their eyes. But we come, at last, out of the town, and instead of taking the direct road to Copenhagen, turn down south towards the German frontier, which is about seventy miles away. An interminable, wet, grey road stretches in front under a leaden sky. But, as soon as Esbjerg is behind us, the prospect alters. The first of the Danish farmhouses comes into view; 'magpie houses', sometimes of but one storey with bright flowers, often geraniums, in the windows; whitewashed houses with a framework of black timber, and thatched roofs. And there are the stepped church towers of Denmark, towers which have almost the look of lighthouses in the distance, and which in many instances stand upon mounds, making one wonder if there are not foundations of earlier pagan wooden temples underneath them. They are brick churches, whitewashed over, and their stepped towers, to be dated between 1450 and 1550, we shall find to have their counterpart in the brick keeps of the early Danish castles. These church towers are a distinctive feature of Denmark and of Skåne, the southern-most province of Sweden, and already, little by little, they begin to give character to the landscape. In nothing, inside or out, do they in the least resemble Dutch churches, neither is the landscape at all like Holland. And to fill in the picture there are the Danish children with their flaxen hair.

In rather less than an hour we are nearing Ribe, which at this moment does not arouse high expectations. Its suburbs, to be truthful, look just like anywhere else upon a rainy day. But the rain begins to glisten from cobbled pavements. There are old houses. Ribe, after all, is going to be worth a visit. And at this instant, like a hybrid of a Chelsea pensioner and Father Christmas, a bearded figure in a red coat rides by upon his bicycle, first of the Danish postmen. They wear the livery of the Royal family, a red subtly different from the old scarlet of the British Army, a red with a touch of yellow in it, so that it is keyed down a bit, an 'off-geranium' without a shade of orange; and the postman's red coat is so much another of the features of Denmark that it is worth trying to fix and identify the colour. Already, as if in compliment, the red brick houses had begun, And they *do* have, here, at last, only an hour after landing at Esbjerg, a character, and at that, the character of Denmark. For Ribe is in Jutland, only just in Jutland. Almost the first thing I noticed after its red brick houses was a travel poster of what must be the yet more fascinating brick buildings of Tønder, a little town an hour further to the south, now on the frontier, but seized by the Prussians in 1863, incorporated into Germany, and only restored to the Danes in 1920. Tønder has, most obviously, a little and distinct character of its own, and may be one of the prettiest of all the red brick towns of Northern Europe. I am sorry not to have seen it, and can only do my best to write of it, and of the island of Fanø, from hearsay, in order to enliven our return to Esbjerg and our last day in Denmark.

The delightful old houses of Ribe seem to be of their own shade of red brick, and I would say they are the colour of half-ripened mulberries. More than one of them looks as though it should have an eighteenth century grenadier in pipeclay uniform, white gaiters, and half-mitre, half-sugar-loaf cap, marching up and down outside its door. Such is the key and indication to its architecture. Being at Ribe during daytime we missed the night watchman in his greatcoat, with spiked staff and lantern, who makes the rounds calling the hours, and, for all I know, gives weather forecasts more accurately than the Air Ministry. Standing alone in midst of the old houses is the cathedral, with an interior of the fifteenth century and some of the fascinating *epitaphia* or Danish

22

wall tombs, rich in heraldry, with incomprehensible inscriptions, and up at the top, nearly out of sight, a painted portrait of the deceased, often with all his family—paintings which are always interesting for costume, but are at times something more than that. In all of the churches of Denmark, as a whole, there could be a few good paintings by Dutch masters among these *epitaphia*. Ribe cathedral is nothing considerable, but it is old and venerable and a part of Denmark. And the other 'sight' of Ribe are the storks who are as much in the tradition of the town as the ravens at the Tower of London, or the bears in the bear-pit at Berne, and who are given every inducement to settle and remain. Two or three of the old houses have specially built frames or platforms on their roofs upon which the storks can make their nests. Only one of these, that August day, was occupied. The stork population, so numerous all over Europe during the Middle Ages, is fast dwindling. During many journeys in Holland I saw but one storks' nest, near Zwolle; storks are few and far between in Alsace; and it is doubtful if there are as many as a thousand nests in Denmark. And when the last stork leaves Ribe its glory will have departed. Nevertheless, this little town gives you all of old Denmark in a cobbled square. And, already, it is apparent that the history of Denmark is its monarchy. This, to a greater extent than any other country in Europe, big or small, excepting Spain. Ribe, with seven thousand inhabitants, about the size of Burford or Chipping Campden, once a seaport, now in the middle of green marshes, although so near to Germany, is typically Danish, all the more so because unlike Copenhagen it has no touch of sophistication from eighteenth century France. There is the knowledge that Ribe is in Southern Jutland and that in this mediaeval town they held obstinately to their inward growing ways. Its old castles and manor houses apart, there is perhaps no place so typical of the quieter side of Denmark. So much so that, even hating noise, one dreads to spend a night there and is happy to move on.

On our way to Odense we now cross the whole neck of Jutland, Jylland, as they call it, which at this point is not quite forty miles wide. We are soon out of the meres and marshes and in gently sloping country among cornfields, pale, not golden cornfields, which are exactly the colour of the children's hair. It is pastoral, but not interesting, and in less than an hour we see the blue Baltic waters of the Little Belt or Sound, just before coming to Kolding, where there is no reason at all to linger, and we go on a few miles passing a large old half-timber eighteenth century inn or posting house to the left of the road which must have been a familiar sight to generations of travellers, having all the time to our right the wooded shores of Fyn, or Funen, the second island of the kingdom. Some of the most beautiful Danish castles and manor houses are on Funen, the most fertile part of Denmark, which is now becoming easier to visualize as consisting of three main parts or divisions; the mainland from the neck upwards being Jutland; then this intermediate or middle island, Funen; and beyond that the principal island, Zealand, or Sjælland, with Copenhagen at its far side on the coast opposite Sweden, and a chain of smaller islands, six or seven in all, reaching in an arc across the Baltic from the mainland to the south of Zealand. These islands are parallel, in fact, to the curve of the German coast from Kiel to Stettin; it being about two hundred miles from the southernmost point of Denmark, at Gedser on the isle of Falster, where we shall be going, up to the fishing village of the Skaw on the narrow spit of land between the Skagerrak and Kattegat, at the entrance to the Baltic. And Denmark at its widest, between Copenhagen and the furthest point of Jutland, is about two hundred and forty miles across. Much of this area is water; but warming up after a slow beginning there will be many things to interest us when we have time to look around.

A huge and splendid bridge now looms up, joining Jutland to Funen, and at the far side of it we are in Middelfart, a town the amenities of which are scarcely improved when the guide book, catering for all tastes, tells us that the Folk Museum is "notable for memories of porpoise hunts and ferry service". And now it is but an hour's drive to Odense, in the middle of the island, through prosperous looking villages and past rich farms. Odense has a hundred thousand inhabitants and is the second town in Denmark. I felt that a previous visit

2, 3 COPENHAGEN
from the Tower of Our
Saviour's (1682–96)

4, 5 (*above*) Details of the *Epitaphium* of Otto Krabbe (*d.* 1719) in Roskilde Cathedral

6 Venetian Glass Figures playing the game of "Morra"

twenty years ago had absolved me from again visiting the house where Hans Christian Andersen was born, and am sure he would have wished it so. It is becoming imperative that the Danes should give Hans Andersen a rest. Have they not Tycho Brahe, Kierkegaard, and other great men? Too much Hans Andersen, even, somewhat spoils Odense. We reached there at about five o'clock in the middle of a mael-strom of bicycles in gently falling rain which soon quickened into a wild downpour. That evening we dined early at *Den Gamle Krø*, with name reminiscent, we thought, of a ballad about a raven, but on enquiry all it means is "the old inn", and it seems scarcely credible that the last gargantuan meal had been on board the *Kronprins Frederik*, lying off Esbjerg, for in the interval we had seen Ribe and been half across Denmark.

In the morning we saw the Church of St. Knud, the largest Gothic church in Denmark, where King Christian II is buried, but with no monument. It has a golden altarpiece of carved wood in the style of Sleswig, rococo organ and pulpit, and the chapel of the Counts of Ahlefeldt, which Marryat calls "a really noble dormitorium". He, also, tells the story of a balletomane lady of the family who danced at a ball in Odense with twelve knights, one after another, and fell exhausted, dead, at the feet of the twelfth knight, her partner. The bodies rest in great coffins like travelling chests, covered with repoussé work in silver, something only to be seen in Denmark and in Sweden. But the chapel is notable for a fine baroque monument, probably by the Dutch sculptor Th. Quellinus, to Hans von Ahlefeldt of Glorup, Lord Lieutenant of Funen, and his two wives and son. There are, in all, some five or six such monuments in Denmark, all of which we hope to notice in their turn, and in every one of them there is a particular and almost comical emphasis upon the periwig, worn whenever excuse allowed with half-armour, and no whit less fantastic and extravagant of appearance than the Turkish Sultans and their turbans. Nowhere else, of which I have knowledge, are the curls of the periwigs so deeply undercut, or their poodle or *caniche*-like effect so honestly portrayed. There are two more quiet and beautiful old churches in

Odense, despite the noise outside, but with nothing much within them, and there is the flower garden of the White Palace, no longer a Royal palace but lived in by the Lord Lieutenant of Funen. And yet . . . without making so abrupt a statement as Horace Marryat, writing ninety-five years ago, who says, "I have done my best to like Odense, but can't!", I would suggest that Odense is little improved, since then. This may be because it is 'the second city' of Denmark, and the second anything at all is never as good as the first, and nearly always inferior to what comes after it. One thing, at least, is certain. Odense is noiser and more full of human beings than it was a hundred years ago.

But if Odense is a disappointment, not so the island of Funen to which we return again, making the results of three or four journeys thither into a composite chapter, and continuing now upon our way to Copenhagen. In half an hour, or hardly as long as that, we come down through the woods and fields to Nyborg, which was to become so familiar through catching the ferry at the last moment, or waiting there for an hour or more, while students offered their services as English guides, and small boys going from car to car asked all and sundry, indiscriminately, to write their autographs in grubby notebooks.

The ferry boat, once on board, is entirely and absolutely immaculate and takes you in less than an hour and a half over the Great Belt to Korsør, on the main island of Zealand, whence it is two hours' run to Copenhagen. That it was not so, once, is witnessed by the old timber frame house in Korsør, with sandstone figures on its front of the four seasons, where the Kings of Denmark had to while away the time, often for days on end, waiting for a favourable wind to cross the Belt. It may be imagined how in mediaeval times this would give opportunity for the 'situation to deteriorate'. A road surface as fine as any in Europe leads across Zealand (Sjæland) and into Copenhagen, but we take the chance of stopping for an hour on the way at Roskilde, sometimes to be seen written in old books, surprisingly, as "Rothschild", and it is here in the cathedral of Roskilde that we apprehend how old and historic a part of Europe is the Danish Kingdom. We see the twin copper spires of Roskilde, and with some difficulty get off the arterial road. It is a red brick building, unexceptional in size, and quite full of tombs of kings and queens; the tomb-chapel of Christian IV, and four tremendous sarcophagi of Frederik IV and Christian V, but until we know more of them it is only muddling to give their names. Other tombs in plenty covered with velvet and silver *repoussé*, down to some which are in pure 'Empire' style; and monuments to less important personages including the *epitaphium* to Otto Krabbe (d. 1719), a pretty piece of baroque of which we illustrate the whole and the detail, also, showing Fame not content with blowing her trumpet but holding a spare one in her hand, flanked by a weeping muse in plumed helm and low cut breastplate, enticingly designed. No hour was striking; so we could not see the mediaeval clock with wooden mechanical figures of St. George and the Dragon. Two figures of bell-ringers strike the hour, the horse rears up, and the dragon "utters a piercing cry of death and despair". But, instead of waiting for that we went to see the lay-convent of Roskilde, our first experience of these uniquely Danish institutions and forerunner of Vallø, of Vemmetofte, and Gisselfeld, and saw therein the banqueting-hall where the ladies dine together at feasts and high festivals, with its hangings of gilt leather, old cabinets, and fading portraits of old kings and queens. Half an hour after that we were in Copenhagen.

CHAPTER II

Copenhagen

THE capital of Denmark has a prevailing or predominant whiteness. Not only are many of its houses, old and new, whole streets of them, painted white, but there is a white quality in the Danish sunlight, with more than a shade in it of the snows of winter. The white paint of the houses is quite different from the yellow stucco of Regent's Park, of Carlton House Terrace, of the squares at Brighton. It is plain white, sometimes with a tint of grey in it. In the better parts of the town, therefore, it is a white capital. So I remembered it from twenty years before, and so again it proved to be driving down the long straight road into the heart of Copenhagen, through the Town Hall Square, parallel to the Strøget or main shopping street, and at last to Kongens Nytorv with the equestrian statue of the King in the middle and the white-painted Hotel d'Angleterre.

It was pleasant in the morning looking out over the clipped trees to King Christian V on his pedestal, a philoprogenitive monarch in true seventeenth century tradition, and over his head to the masts and white-painted hulls of the shipping in Nyhavn, a canal or arm of the harbour which comes right into the far corner of the square. A drawback is the noisiness of the square at night, but one forgets that on a fine morning when drinking the Danish coffee and eating a Danish almond cake. These latter appear with a miraculous freshness every morning, hot and crisp, and must be among the most delicious things it is possible to eat for breakfast.*

* Made in the kitchens of the hotel, I would have thought, but a recent book mentions "one of Denmark's two most famous bakeries

30

They are certainly better for one than the *brioches* and *croissants* of Paris, and henceforth the taste of almond will remind one always of Copenhagen.

Perhaps the best and most obvious thing to do on the first morning is to walk round the Kongens Nytorv past the eighteenth century Thotts Palais, now the French Embassy, at the corner, and along the Bredgade to the Amalienborg. It is a little like arriving in Rome and rushing immediately to St. Peter's in order to see the Swiss Guard in their striped uniforms on guard between Bernini's columns. And taking the turning to the right of the Bredgade, opposite the domed Marble Church, we are in a moment in one of the loveliest eighteenth century squares in Europe, with the four palaces of the Amalienborg spreading diamond-wise before us, connected by their colonnades. Sentries of the Danish Life Guard are on duty, pacing up and down holding their rifles in front of them with two hands, but not in full dress uniform, for the Royal Family are away. And taking but a perfunctory look at the architecture, for we are to spend four weeks in Copenhagen, we walk out of the square, down the quiet and white Amaliegade, and so back to the hotel. Likewise in the afternoon, for we arrive at Rosenborg Castle by a misunderstanding at three o'clock when it is about to close, and we are only in time to go in at the door where are the red-coated attendants in the Royal livery, walk round the ground floor rooms in a hurry and come out again. Perhaps it is better so on the first day, when there are mornings and afternoons, enough, and to spare.

Neither is it in the least necessary to take in the whole of the famous and beautiful Tivoli Gardens at a first experience. At any time of life one could spend a whole summer day, and up to midnight, there. For nothing in Europe is quite like the Tivoli. As we entered that evening the Italian pantomime was playing, or just ending, and we were in time to hear the

(*Konditorei*) where the famous almond cakes are made which appear on all the best tables in the country ". This is at Kolding, just before the bridge to Funen (see p. 24). The other *Konditorei* is at Aalborg, see *Holiday in Denmark with Bon Viveur*, Frederick Muller Ltd., 1955, pp. 25, 64.

chorus of children calling for Pierrot, "to say something".
And it came on to rain, and we had to hurry off to dinner at
the *Belle Terrasse*, one of the four or five good restaurants
within the gardens. It would be well advised to dine and spend
the evening of every night in Tivoli, and there is every objec-
tion to exploring and spoiling it all upon this first occasion.

But next morning, and for two successive mornings, we
went to Rosenborg Castle and saw it all in detail. It is a dark
brick building that we have to consider as being, once, of
bright red brick, a building about the size of the keep of
Bolsover Castle, no bigger, or since many readers will not
know Bolsover, let us say, about as big as a large old manor
house in England. But it is of Bolsover that it reminds us,
although Bolsover is built of stone. This is a question of
atmosphere and 'feeling', for Rosenborg is, in fact, a typical
Dutch Renaissance building with its red brick and sandstone
dressings. A Dutchman, Hans Steenwinckel, was architect.
But the long gallery on the third floor where are the chief
treasures of Rosenborg must be an idea borrowed from
houses in England. The interior is an enchantment from top to
bottom, its official listing as the Chronological Collection of
the Danish Kings giving but a faint promise of the fairy tale
treasures and fantasies within. For the Rosenborg alone is
worth the trip to Denmark. We have certainly nothing to
compare with it in England. And nothing quite of its sort
exists in Italy, Germany, or France. There is the same sensation of being in a private collection as in the Prado, but then
the Rosenborg contains no Grecos, Titians, Goyas. It is the
collection of treasures of the Northern Kings with Norway
and Iceland and Greenland in their dominions. That is the
sense in which to look at the Rosenborg, keeping that always
in mind, as much so as one should remember it is the home of
Oriental Sultans and eunuchs when seeing the Old Seraglio at
Istanbul, or that the fountains and terraces of Versailles were
made for the progresses of a Sun King. The Kings of Denmark were at a distance from the great arts of Italy, but their
wealth and absolute power, and a heredity as curious as that
of Habsburg or Bourbon, made it that they were able to
surround their persons with objects as far fetched and fantas-

7, 8 (*above*) Pierrot and Harlequin, in the Tivoli Gardens

9 (*left*) Columbine, Pierrot and Harlequin at foot of the statue of Niels Henrik Volkersen, the original Pierrot of the Tivoli Gardens

10   King Christian IV (1588–1648)

From the portrait by Abraham Wuchters

tic as themselves. It is only just a hundred years ago that
their treasures were installed and put on view here after the
disastrous fire at Frederiksborg. But, somehow, it does not
bear the date of that. And yet another enchantment is the
manner in which the interest does not diminish from floor to
floor as you go upstairs. It is only that times change, as during
the hundred years slumber of the Sleeping Beauty, and then
for a last act or apotheosis the spell begins all over again with
the silver lions and throne of sea-ivory in the Knight's Hall
on the top floor.

We go to the Rosenborg to learn the history of Denmark
and become familiar with the Northern Kings. And the first,
and *pater familias*, is King Christian IV (1588–1648), brother
of Anne of Denmark, and therefore uncle to our Charles I.
Nothing in the Dane seems to have entered into his nephew,
as regards his physical heredity, but Charles must have
inherited his taste from him, and as patron of Inigo Jones, of
Rubens and Van Dyck, have improved upon that. The
Stuart, in spite of his wonderful flair for pictures and probably because of his artistic temperament, had all the obstinate
instability of his race, whereas King Christian was cast,
physically, in a larger mould, was more dependable, and not
only began, but finished things. His physical appearance
quickly becomes one of the familar sights of Denmark,
not least because of his 'marlok'. This is like a pigtail hanging
down the right side of his head, and often tied up with a red
bow. For the King had become afflicted by a horrible hair
disease called *plica polonica*, "a long mat of hair like a
horse's tail distended with blood", which could not be cut
off, and got larger as he grew older. He, therefore, wore this
long lock of hair tied up with ribbon, and 'marloks' were
worn by his courtiers in compliment to him. Christian IV
also lost an eye in a naval battle. He was married, of course,
but we hear little of his Queen and more of his morganatic
wife Christina Munk, "a fine woman with a milkmaid face
and gold-powdered hair", as Marryat calls her, who had
access to many Royal portraits long ago destroyed by fire.
But, in the end, Christina Munk was accused by the King of
infidelity, in front of his Council in this very garden of

Rosenborg, acquitted, but sent into exile in Jutland, prayers were no longer said for her in churches, and the King consoled himself with Christina's tire-woman. Christina Munk was lucky to escape the fate of Ann Boleyn.

Many objects belonging to this typical King of the Northern Renaissance are at Rosenborg, and indeed his rooms can have been little altered since he built them. There is an elaborate and intricate drinking cup representing him in a plumed hat tilting at the ring, And in the next room, his bedroom and one of the earliest instances of *chinoiserie* decoration,* is his magnificent saddle and horse-cloths of black velvet embroidered with gold and pearls, trappings worthy of a Sultan or a Shah of Persia. Many other and lovely baubles of his reign, including badges of the "Armed Hand" or mailed arm in green enamel with diamonds, which Christian gave only to his favourites to wear round their necks, and jewelled badges of the Elephant, of which more anon.

Next come the rooms of Frederik III, a more shadowy figure, but there is no lessening of objects of art and *virtú*. In particular, a fantastic set of masked figures in Venetian enamel, like figures from Callot's engravings, playing the Venetian game of *morra*, the work of some highly stylized and unknown master.† There are, as well, beautiful ship models in ivory carved by the King's armourer, with a poetical beauty in the bellying of their white, almost transparent sails. After a time such objects are more rewarding than indifferent pictures by bad painters. Among the wonders of Rosenborg are the old clothes and dresses. There are suits and uniforms dating from the reigns of Christian IV and Frederik III in glass cases in the entrance passage, and a large quantity of others are put away and not on view.‡

* Curiously there is an early *chinoiserie* room of just this character at Bolsover Castle.

† The game of *morra*, which is still played by Italian children, consists in guessing the number of fingers held out by one's opponent.

‡ The clothes and old dresses at Rosenborg have been made the subject of a learned study, *Kongedragterne from 17 og 18 aarhundrede*, by S. Flamand Christensen, Copenhagen, 1940. It is perhaps the most complete collection of the kind in Northern Europe, and invaluable from the point of view of historical research.

Christian V was first of the Absolute Kings, an anomaly which persisted in Denmark with public support as a curb upon the nobles until the year 1848. It is this King of whom .there is the equestrian statue in the Kongens Nytorv, and it is perhaps typical that it is in him that the dynastic peculiarities of the Kings of the house of Oldenburg first become fixed, to continue until the extinction of the line in 1863. For they developed from somewhere or other, no authority seems to know how or when, a kind of fusion of the Guelph blue eyes and Habsburg chin. This was to reach to extraordinary proportions in the next century when the Royal portraits that are always found in every Danish country house exhibit the strangest dynastic physiognomies that it is possible to imagine. There are the beginnings of it in Christian V. And in the next few reigns the quasi-Habsburg was supplemented with the blue eyes of the Guelph through several intermarriages with our Hanoverian Kings. Christian V, like an absolute monarch in a fairy story, fathered a family *à la main gauche*, his offspring according to the picturesque Danish custom being given the title Gyldenløve (golden lion) in the first generation,* their mother being Sophia Moth, daughter of the Royal physician. Of the two Gyldenløves, her sons, Molesworth says with no trace of surprise and not a raised eyebrow (but then Charles II reigned in England), "The young gentlemen are handsome and hopeful, and looked upon as necessary ornaments to the crown." To these children and their descendants the King gave the title of Excellency, precedence over the other nobles, an extra fleuron on their coronets, and permission to put their servants into the red livery of the Royal Family.

But this is enough of Danish history for one morning. We shall meet their great King Christian IV again at the castle of Frederiksborg, when we begin to go out into the country. That, too, will be the place to speak of the Knights of the

* Given the title Danneskjold (*shield of Denmark*) in the following generation, and the island of Samsø as their appanage. The still flourishing family of Danneskjold-Samsø are descended from one of the sons, and are the only surviving relics of so many Gyldenløves in Danish history.

Elephant. Another of his buildings which keeps constantly
coming into view in Copenhagen is his Stock Exchange or
Børsen, more like a line of warehouses, with copper roof and
eight huge gables, much resembling the Meat Hall at Haarlem, for it is in full blown Dutch Renaissance, but given an
extra touch of fantasy by its tall spire made of four inter-
twining dragons' tails. And finally, a little way out of the
main part of the town, one often passes a whole quarter of
little yellow houses built by the King for his sailors, and once
holding six hundred families. It is now reduced in area but
still lived in by non-commissioned officers in the Royal Navy.
The character of the little houses is half married-quarters,
half almshouses, but looking closer you will see they date
from three hundred years ago.

On any day, or every day in Copenhagen, there is a large
choice of different restaurants for luncheon. Always preceded
by a glass or two of akvavit, from Aalborg in the north of
Jutland, while distracted, it may be, by a menu the size of
the middle pages from an American Sunday newspaper.
There is no doubt that herring is the basic or staple food of
Denmark. In the past, Danish economy depended on the
herring as much as that of Portugal upon *bacalhoa* (cod), but
at least the Danes did not have to go as far as the banks of
Newfoundland for it. With the Baltic on one side of the
country, and the North Sea on the other, they could fish the
shoals from two sides, and the greatest disasters to Denmark
in the Middle Ages were not poor harvests but migrations of
the herring. Smoked eels, as in Holland, are not less popular
than herring, but in this fish-diet kingdom where the gourmet
might look forward to his smoked salmon it is to be noted
that it never equals that from Scotland.* If a complaint may
be heard, it is directed against the monumental slabs of

* The gourmand in me makes me remark that the best smoked
salmon I have ever tasted was on the Alta-fjord in Northern Norway.
But the knowledge that it was smoked by Lapps in their national
costume may have helped in this. Salmon of fifty and even sixty
pounds, the size and weight of small boys ten years old, are not
uncommon in the river Alta. The island of Bornholm is chief source of
Danish salmon.

bread and butter relished by the Danes, but a little repellent to English tastes. There is the famous Oskar Davidsen's sandwich emporium, indeed capital of the world's sandwiches; and there are the two fish restaurants, nearly next door to each other, opposite the Christiansborg Palace, on the Gammel Strand, with a basement shop, below one of them, where are sold woollen jerseys from the Faroe Islands, sabbatarian versions of our Fair Isle sweaters, for they are knitted in dark greys and creams. The fish market is here, with attendant fishwives, and fine and beautiful old houses full of character stretch along the quay. Perhaps this and the more aristocratic Amaliegade are the true old Copenhagen of the merchants and the richer families, both with shipping nearly touching them and seagulls where most towns have pigeons. But one knows all the time that Copenhagen has more than a million inhabitants, and that these older buildings which interest us can mean little or nothing to young families living in workmen's flats in the new suburbs of the town. On the other hand there is so little poverty, as that is understood in Southern Italy, or Spain, or even parts of France, and the level of education and commonsense is so high, that Denmark is probably the most socially contented country in Europe. One has the certainty that the Danes do not resent their past and that more and more of them, as with us in England, derive pleasure from it.

If we now return to Rosenborg in the afternoon, or the following morning, it is to complete the history of Denmark in studying her Kings. Continuing where we left off, we come to a glass case in the middle of the room, holding the Regalia and the Crown Jewels. Here is the crown of Christian IV, first worn by him in 1596, of gold and pearl and enamels, and so intricate and beautiful in workmanship that it is, at first, difficult to tell its date, and it is just, basically, a King's crown in the tradition of crowns from early pagan days. Then, in its filigree lightness and fantasy it becomes a crown of the Renaissance, we remember the same King's saddle and horse-clothes of velvet embroidered with pearls, and that in addition to being a great builder he was a music lover and brought over John Dowland from England to be his lutenist and song writer, paying him, so it is always said, a salary equal to that of the prime minister. The glass case blazes with sapphires and diamonds; an exquisite necklace of Queen Sophie-Magdalene still worn by the reigning queen; Orders of the Dannebrog and of the Elephant; the Orb and Sceptre; the Queen's Crown of rare elegance; and the Crown of the Absolute Kings, of bulbous form and utmost fantasy, exactly designed to wear upon a periwig, worn by them at the coronations until 1840, and in our imagination entirely resembling the crown of King Florestan XXIV in *La Belle au Bois dormant*.*

On the first floor there is a delightful and bewildering plethora of bric-à-brac; golden toilet sets; clocks shaped like pyramids; watches and miniatures; chandeliers; Florentine mosaic work; and two objects, the 'Eider Cup', and another gold cup, both made to celebrate the abduction of Anna Sophie Reventlow from the Castle of Clausholm by the Absolute King, who at the time was married and had his other wife still living. We put it, thus, in order to heighten the interest, because our plan in this present work is to touch upon subjects lightly, merely introducing a name or a theme till we become familiar with it, and when occasion serves, returning to it again. The Absolute King in question was Frederik IV (1699–1730), and this is our introduction to what Horace Marryat so rightly calls *le front fuyant*, for that has never perhaps been so much exemplified in any human being as in this strange looking monarch. We shall see the extraordinary painting of him at Frederiksborg,† and will in time visit beautiful and remote Clausholm with its marvellous

* The crown of Christian IV, being an elected King, is "open"; that of Christian V, an hereditary and absolute King, is "closed". The beautiful sceptre of Christian V is shaped like a light blue lily supporting a crown of enamelled gold and diamonds.

† A small and delightful bad painting at Rosenborg of his Coronation shows a negro page holding his favourite dog, a huge mastiff or 'Great Dane' upon a lead. The page had orders to hold him still, but when the primate was about to place the King's Crown upon his head the dog sprang from his keeper, rushed to the King, and placed his forepaws on the Royal knees, snarling and baring his teeth to the bishop and would only be pacified by the King.

stucco ceilings. From now onwards the Royal physiognomy grows more far fetched and peculiar in every generation; verging on madness; achieving that, in the person of Christian VII, married to a Princess of Great Britain; and recovering in the martinet-like form and military tread of Frederik VI, not the least Habsburg-looking of them all with his pale hair, blue eyes, and jutting chin. A portrait of him in the uniform of the Life Guards gives us the likeness of this anachronistic counterpart to Philip IV or Charles II of Spain, for he died as recently as 1839. Of Frederik VII, last King of the old line, there are a pair of delightful *Biedermeier* paintings showing him entering Copenhagen on his wedding day in 1841, greeted by an admiring crowd and treading a red carpet between long files of soldiery. This, too, with its companion painting, seems as far off now as a wedding from a fairy story, and it is amusing to be told that the chamberlain walking with such dignity in front of the Royal pair had in the King's opinion attracted too much attention to himself and eclipsed his master, with result that the painter had to start all over again and omit his figure in the second version. They are pictures which belong to a particular and neglected school, Royal and military scenes of 1820 to 1850 to be found in corners of Royal palaces all over Europe and, indifferently, in Berlin, Vienna, Naples, Madrid, but probably most of all, St. Petersburg. In my own memory I have pendants to them from the Casa del Labrador at Aranjuez, the Casita del Principe at the Escorial, and the Royal Palace of Caserta, but it may be that the wedding procession of Prince Frederik and Princess Marianne of Mecklenburg-Strelitz is prize-winner of the whole school.* This palace in a fairy tale ends with photographs showing Queen Alexandra as Princess

---

* Frederik VII was married three times, his third and morganatic wife being the ballerina Louise Rasmussen, later created Countess Danner. Rooms occupied by them, with contemporary furniture, are to be seen at the castle of Jægerspris on the Roskilde-fjord, about thirty miles north of Copenhagen. Although last of the old line of the house of Oldenburg, Frederik VII, the cousin of his predecessor Christian VIII, bowed to the democratic precepts of 1848 and was never crowned as Absolute King. He died in 1863, and was succeeded by Christian IX, father of our Queen Alexandra, and first of the new

of Wales in all her beauty, family groups with the giant Tsar Alexander III, and such little and intriguing objects as the programme from a gala performance of the Royal Danish Ballet at some date in the '80's or 90's of last century with a drawing of a golden coach being drawn along with ropes of flowers by children of the ballet school dressed as *heyducks*. And these heyducks, of whom more later, who appear at Court ceremonies in Denmark with pots of artificial flowers in their half-sugarloaf hats, were among the minor mysteries I came to Copenhagen to enquire into.

After which we once more climb the spiral stone stair and come up into the Knights' Hall upon the third floor, occupying nearly the whole of that and reminiscent, as we have said, of the long galleries in Elizabethan houses. There is silver furniture, but above all there are the three silver lions, dating from 1670, and in pure descent from the lions of the Byzantine Throne Room. The Throne is of narwhal tusks; while, as for the lions, they now stand at the King's feet in the House of Commons when he reads a speech of national importance. In smaller cabinets leading out of the Knights' Hall are a complete collection of the Flora Danica porcelain; a room arranged in the seventeenth century to hold Venetian glass given to Frederik IV of 'le front fuyant' by the Doge of Venice, in fact, a cavern or ornamental grotto of glass; and rare Persian *polonaise* carpets woven with silver in colours of pale green and almond and pistachio. Coming down from the Knights' Hall and out of the Rosenborg, and looking back at it, one may wonder where else in the world all the history of a little and ancient kingdom can be learnt from little and precious baubles, all within four walls of an old brick castle. In the whole collection there is nothing at all that is sinister and frightening, and perhaps not the least remarkable feature is that although in arrangement it dates from rather over a hundred years ago it does not bear that signature of time upon it. Indeed, the Chronological Collection of the Danish Kings appears to have put itself in order as every

line of Kings. The apparently simple, but in fact very perplexing alternation of Christians and Frederiks upon the throne of Denmark, had its beginning in Christian I (1448–1481) and Frederick I (1523–1533).

11 (*above*) The Wedding
Procession of Frederik
VII, headed by the Court
Chamberlain, Count
Lewetzau (1842)
*From the painting by Chr.
Baalsgaard*

12 (*left*) Frederik VI in
uniform of a Danish in-
fantry regiment, walking
in the gardens of
Frederiksberg (*c.* 1813)
*From a gouache by Johan-
nes Senn* (1780–1861)

14 Crown of King Christian IV, the Goldsmith Diderik Furien (d. 16 and his working jeweller Corvinia Sauer

15 Jewelled Badge of the Order of Elephant (about 1650)

13 A Court Heyduck in uniform

reign ended, from the time of Christian IV until half a
century ago.

There is a short cut through the Rosenborg gardens
whence may be heard bugling and stamping from the Danish
Life Guard, and walking past the flower beds and the weeping
willows for something to think of let us talk of Horace
Marryat. It is a commonplace that there is always an Englishman who has been everywhere, and he is an instance. His
book, *A Residence in Jutland, the Danish Isles and Copenhagen*, was published in two volumes by John Murray in 1860.
He was the brother of Captain Marryat of *Midshipman Easy*,
but, that apart, an aura of mystery surrounds him. From
internal evidence he was at school at Eton. When his
book came out he was forty or fifty years old, but we know
neither how he occupied his time till then, nor how and why
he came to Denmark. One story is that he had run away with
the wife of an English bishop, while another story says that
his companion in exile was an English duchess. Whatever the
truth, he was travelling 'in style' with carriages and ladies'
maids and English schoolboys who came out on holiday. The
Royal Family showed him hospitality and entertained him,
which would hardly have occurred in the case of an ordinary,
undistinguished traveller as, for instance, when he writes:
"When I first went to Frederiksborg his Majesty" (Frederik
VII, d. 1863, of the wedding procession) "graciously invited
me to remain on a visit, and the following morning did me
the honour to show me the collection in person." During the
great fire at the castle which Marryat describes so well, "As
his Majesty descended the steps on his way to the carriage he
stayed for one moment to greet me . . . and kindly pressed my
hand." There is probably justification for thinking that it was
because of his exalted companion, or companions, that
Horace Marryat was received. In the apostrophe at the end
of this book he extols Denmark as a place "for those more
advanced in life—who have been everywhere and have done
everything—who abominate being whirled for pleasure
across the fair face of Europe by a locomotive" (feelings
which I, myself, share with him where aeroplanes are concerned, and which put me in the same 'age group'!). What is

remarkable in Horace Marryat is his appreciation of the past, in particular of the seventeenth century, a period so little understood in mid-Victorian times, and his store of curious and unsuspected information. He had, also, the gift of phrase; though I would say that some of his phrases, *le front fuyant*, or in another place where he writes of "long *effilé* hands", where he writes, again, of "a black mask similar to those worn at the *bal masqué*, minus the *bavolet*", or tells of "an Oriental type of countenance—long dark eyes *fendu à l'amande*" betray the conversation of his companion, and that this companion spoke the *lingua franca* of high born ladies of the Regency. Letters of ladies of that generation are full of these French phrases, and nothing could be further removed from the language written and spoken by his brother, the author of *Midshipman Easy*. On all accounts I wish we knew more of Horace Marryat. But only one or two Englishmen have troubled to read him, and except in one instance that I know of he is unread by the Danes.

Yet Marryat tells us exactly what we most want to hear about Denmark. Not only her ancient history, but descriptions of her country houses. Certain of his passages, such as that describing the fire at Frederiksborg, stay in the memory with something of poetry, while it is Marryat who initiates us into the minor but enchanted world of Gyldenløves, and inspires us to look for portraits, if such there are, of the diamonded lay-abbesses of Gisselfeld and Vallø. The only, and curious omission in Marryat is any mention of the heyducks. But, in almost every other instance, where anything interesting or sensible is to be said, he says it. And perhaps the only other necessary guide, apart from using one's own eyes, is Lurids de Thurah's *Den Danske Vitruvius*, the eighteenth century book of engravings of Danish palaces and other buildings. Having apostrophized Denmark, Marryat moved to Sweden, but his book on that country though full, as we would expect, of interesting bits of information is long winded and a little flat. He had become too crotchety, and the use, or misuse of the cuspidor was the plaint upon his mind. He writes horrifying, onomatapoeic imitations of spitting, objects to smoking, and emerges at the end of it like a literary aunt or elder sister of Augustus Hare. But in Denmark, and among the Danes, Horace Marryat was in his prime. And I would suggest, now, that with him still in mind we continue on our tour of Copenhagen.

There is, for instance, the Royal Palace of Christiansborg, on the island just across the water from the Gammel Strand. Not so much for what it is, now, which with all respect is the Danish Foreign Office, as for what it was before, and for an interest, it may be, once, more animal than human. For here were the Royal Mews and the Riding School or Manège with, in Marryat's day, "the white horses, true albinos with roseate eyes and ears, used by the King on State occasions". And he continues, "When these cream-coloured horses came into fashion I cannot say; Christian V (the first of the Absolute Kings) drove light iron-greys with black heads, tails, and manes", the truth being that these came from the famous stud at the castle of Frederiksborg, outside the capital. The Kings of Denmark had long been great amateurs of horses, a cult that found much favour, too, with German princes, as witness the white and the cream ponies (Isabellas) of the Electors of Hanover, and the 'tigered' horses of the Grand Dukes of Oldenburg, the cream-coloured ponies that drew the English Coronation coach being descended from the former. Horses of this 'true albino breed' were presented to the giant Tsar Alexander III by his brother-in-law Christian IX, and at the great annual review of the Imperial Guard at Krasnoye-Selo towards the end of August the Gospodina (sister of our Queen Alexandra) drove out to the inspection with her ladies in a carriage drawn by eight of these white horses with pink eyes and ears. Now the breed is extinct, or all but extinct.* As for Christiansborg Palace, like all other Danish palaces, it has been burnt down again and

* A Spanish 'pen-friend' of the author, in his splendid book, *A los Colores del Caballo*, by Miguel Odriozola, Madrid, Publicaciones del Sindicato Nacional de Ganadería, 1951, describes these horses, pp. 136–138, and illustrates, in colour, a stallion of the breed, *pelaje blanco piel-rosa*, and it has, in fact, a roseate tint in its skin. He informed me in a letter that he had recently visited Denmark and found some surviving traces of these horses, which were something other than mere albinos.

47

again, this being the sixth palace to stand upon the site. In its heyday it had been one of the buildings of Queen Sofia Madalena of Brandenburg-Bayreuth, a German princess who in Marryat's words "from very weariness launched out into extravagance", but then, as he reminds us, "she was not only the wife of an absolute sovereign, but also the wife of one of the most consummate bores that ever existed" (Christian VI). This Queen with some shades in her of the Empress Catherine, but uneducated, we shall meet again as the founder of lay convents, but, as well, she built the enormous, and one would think, beautiful palace of Hirschholm, also destroyed, but in fact it was pulled down and its contents sold. It is a wonder, in fact, that any works of art from the Royal palaces have survived. Christiansborg, as it now stands, is nearly if not entirely new, while the old Riding School is now the Theatrical Museum wherein the balletomane may look for old prints and early photographs of Bournonville. What still remains is the old Court Theatre and, more charming still, the rococo marble bridge and its pair of pavilions crossing an arm of the canal, and making one more regretful still for Sofia Madalena's palace before it was burnt down. Here also is the great hall of the Arsenal with dozens of bronze cannon, and upstairs, under the eye of military veterans in red coats, splendid military uniforms including the entire outfit, silver breastplate, silver helmet with double eagle, and all, of an officer of the Tsar's Chevaliers Gardes, a sight for eyes weary of gas-mask and battle dress.

Coming out of Christiansborg the other way, not the rococo bridge end, one is near one of the finest churches in Copenhagen, the Holmen's Kirken. Here are buried Niels Juel and other naval heroes in the usual huge travelling trunks, all velvet and repoussé, and it is still the church of the Danish Navy and the Royal Family. And now there are a few moments for walking down the Strøget and looking in shop-windows. It is the Bond Street or Faubourg St. Honoré of Copenhagen made memorable, so far as I am concerned, by a family of Greenlanders in full national dress, the women in high sealskin boots and trousers and jackets worked with coloured beads, like Fair Isle sweaters, but in glass instead

16, 17, 18 At Odense (*top*), Frÿdenlund (*centre*) and Sorgenfreÿ
All from Lurids de Thurah "Den Danske Vitruvius" (1746–49)

ROYAL PALACES

19, 20 Ceilings in the Queen's Audience Chamber
at Frederiksberg (1724)
C. H. Brenno, stuccoist

of wool. There are all the shops one would expect of a modern capital in the Strøget with one or two more thrown in, as, for example, the Royal Danish Porcelain showrooms where one may buy, at a price, replicas of the Flora Danica service,* and many other and less expensive things including services of Meissen character, and more modern works, seagulls in grey skies, polar bears, figures of children, and so forth, the regular Copenhagen porcelain, in fact. Danish silver, too, of course, and chemist's shops and scent shops; wax-candle shops, which seem to be a speciality of Denmark, with every form and colour of candle imaginable, down to nursery night lights; flower shops with the accent on indoor plants; grocers with the 'national' herring displayed in quantity; and usually in basements, cheese shops with ordinary 'blue' and rarer Samsø cheese.

One so soon gets used to the tempo and rhythm of living in Copenhagen, which is not much different than the contrast between, say, Edinburgh and London. Some persons, of course, would say that hotel life is not the same as living in the bosom of a Danish family, but that is equivalent to denying that you have in fact been to any town where you have only lived in an hotel. Were that so, how few of us have really been to Rome or Paris! It would seem that there are but two ways; you stay in an hotel, or remain for months and learn the language. In any case, a book which is more about Denmark than about the Danes requires that we should see as many of the sights as possible, walk about and around Copenhagen and enter its old courts and churches.

For wet days of which there were several, even in August, there are the galleries and museums, and especially, because it is unique, the National Museum. There is nothing here to

* Wilfrid Blunt in *The Art of Botanical Illustration*, London, Collins & Co., 1950, pp. 166, 167, tell us its history. T. Holmskjold, director of the Copenhagen porcelain factory, a pupil of Linnaeus and a keen botanist, persuaded the Crown Prince of Denmark to commission a table-service in which each piece would be decorated with a plant copied from the *Flora Danica*, an immense botanical publication of drawings of Danish flora. It was begun in 1790, but discontinued in 1802 after two thousand pieces had been produced.

compare with the Viking boats of Oslo with prows curved like swans' necks and marvellous and intricate objects of carved wood on board, but there is a glass case full of bronze horns or *lurs*, enough instruments indeed for a brass band, and only one other extant specimen outside the museum, at Wedellsborg in Funen. These horns, dating from the Late Bronze Age (*c.* 500 B.C.), are always found lying in bogs, always in pairs as though they are man and wife, and each pair always tuned to the same note. Some of the *lurs* can still be played; they give a low resonant note, and were used as war horns in pagan ceremonies. There are, as well, a pair of horned helmets of bronze, also found in a bog; and all the bog-burials which are of a fascinating interest because of the Bronze Age clothes, mostly of brown and black wool. From a millennium and a half later there are the clothes of the Greenland Norsemen, dating from the thirteenth century when there were in West Greenland three hundred farms, fourteen churches, two monasteries, and a bishop. These are the only mediaeval daily garments in existence; long coats with hoods attached, the peak of the hood falling in a long tail behind almost to the waist. They are, in fact, the working clothes of Dante or of Chaucer. And not long after, the last ship came out from Denmark; the Greenland Norsemen were cut off. They became dwarfed and degenerate through intermarriage, and terrible to think of, died out, one by one.*

In the galleries there are French Impressionist paintings, particularly by Gauguin, who married a Danish lady; and

* Probably soon after 1500. But there is an early travellers' tale of a ship sailing off Greenland, some fifty years later, and a man coming out of a hut or tent and looking towards them. He may have been last of the whole race. The Eskimos had not yet arrived. They came soon after and took possession of West Greenland. For many years until the beginning of this century it was thought there might be survivors of the Vikings in East Greenland. Whatever their degree of isolation it could not have been more extreme than that of the four hundred Eskimo inhabitants of Thule, in West Greenland, who, when discovered about seventy years ago, thought they were the only living beings. Now, it is an enormous U.S.A. air base, and their silence and solitude are ended.

something a little more specialized in the form of paintings by the Danish school of 1820–40; delightful in the home scene, but at their best when the painters had drunk of Italian sunlight and gone down south to Rome and Naples. They form a little compact school of their own, much relished by the Danes but hardly known outside Denmark. And there is Thorvaldsen, who came home from Italy to Copenhagen like a conquering hero, and who as an antithesis to modern sculpture is as remote and far removed as the Eskimos of Thule. Nothing could be further from the canons of modern taste than his *Three Graces*. They are of another world from Henry Moore or Giacometti. Which will survive the other is a matter for the reader to decide for himself, but we have to consider looking at 'modern' sculptures in a hundred years from now when works of art have lasted by their intrinsic quality. Then, Thorvaldsen may still be cold and chilly, but while his admirers may be lukewarm other tastes and admirations may have turned to hate.

It is, of course, the classicism of the time of Thorvaldsen which has given to Copenhagen a little touch of classical St. Petersburg. For there is nothing of Berlin in Copenhagen; no Unter den Linden, or Brandenburger Tor. But there *is*, surely, something of St. Petersburg. The streets of white houses? The fortresses and palaces on islands? Not, certainly, the population. But the sunlight, and the long winters? Everything, of course, upon a smaller scale. Would not all Russians have loved the entertainments in the Tivoli? The Italian pantomime which had its exact counterpart in the *balagani* players? Russians living in Copenhagen have told me how much it reminded them of St. Petersburg. They could not say, exactly, in what, but it is like a smaller St. Petersburg without the slums and without the *moujiks*. Like an ideal section of St. Petersburg with, of course, the Court Opera and Ballet. Perhaps not so much like St. Petersburg, as like what they would have liked St. Petersburg to be, without its heartlessness and huge open spaces. There is never a moment of confusion between Stockholm and Copenhagen, and too much love was lost between the two countries in the past to allow one to copy the other even in the smallest ways.

But, above all, Stockholm is a town in an archipelago of little islands, whereas Copenhagen is a town holding a strait or narrow passage of sea. It is the capital city at the entrance to the Baltic, and an ancient community of interests put it apart from Prussia and from Sweden, and perhaps gave it some little points of resemblance to the capital of Peter the Great at the far end of the landlocked sea.

Nothing in Copenhagen is more agreeable than a walk to Christianshavn, though the perpetual repetition of Fredrik and Christian makes the nomenclature as limited as the Achmets and Mahomets of North Africa and Egypt; unless the reader would care to guess for himself who was the builder of Christianshavn, and if he guesses Christian IV he is correct. It is the old harbour quarter of Copenhagen, and it is full of old houses except along its modern main street. It has one church, Christian's Church, with an interior like a theatre. That is to say, the audience are disposed in grand tiers and upper circles, but sadly, the interior is painted grey, not golden, and is decidedly *not* in Bibiena taste, being more adapted to retired seafaring-folk and being for that reason just a little reminiscent of the white sailors' church at Whitby, except that it is far less cheerful. But the attraction of Christianshavn is the canal when that is full of fishing boats drawn up stem to stern. These craft still have a wonderful complexity of ropes and rigging, and the canal bank is a place to wander for an hour or two. Nearly every house in this quarter is an old house; and there are larger buildings, a Naval Hospital, and the warehouses of the former Danish East Asiatic Company which managed the few isolated Danish settlements on the Gulf of Guinea, and further away still on the coast of Coromandel.* Here, too, across the main

* The late Robert Byron told the writer of his visit to the former Danish settlement of Frederiksnagore, of the stone lions of Denmark still guarding the gateway of the fort, and of two old Danish ladies still living in retirement there. This was in about 1930. Denmark gave up her settlement at Frederiksnagore in 1845. The Danish West Indian islands of St. Croix, St. Thomas, and St. John passed to the United States by purchase in 1916. The Danes had bought St. Croix, pronounced San Croy, most inexplicably from the Knights of Malta. Patrick Leigh Fermor in his *The Traveller's Tree*, London, John Murray, 1950, pp.

street and its bicycles is Heering's Gård where the cherry brandy is made, its whole courts and buildings permeated with the smell of cherries, cherries arriving in great wooden barrels from the country, cherry stones in process of crushing, down to the new machinery which corks the bottles and even, obligingly, puts the labels on. But the Church of Our Saviour is not far away with its exceedingly curious copper lighthouse spire, looking as though a Dutch architect had made a study of the steeples of Wren's City churches and decided to 'go one better'. In the result the spire, but the spire only, is as fantastic in design as any building of the school of Borromini, and indeed resembles the lighthouse spire by Calamech for one of the destroyed churches of Messina.* It is, at once, like a lighthouse and like a telescope, with spiral staircase going up outside it instead of hidden in the interior, the ornament of the tower being the staircase balustrading. The sightseer who cannot be bothered to enter misses the most interesting church interior in Copenhagen. A high altar of nearly Spanish exuberance, and an organ loft almost Mexican in fantasy and execution, except that it is in plain wood and does not glitter with the gold of Mexico. The subject is foliage and elephants, in honour of the Order of the Elephant, which had been reconstituted about then by the reigning monarch Christian V. The other interior feature is the font, again as if fonts by Grinling Gibbons and other craftsmen in the London churches had been studied with the view of surpassing them. It is formed of white marble cherubs, with a golden cover hanging over it, with a full quiverful of more cherubs lined up in wood to lift the balustrade.

The confusion of Frederiks and Christians makes it

237–239, describes a visit to this group, known as the Virgin Islands, and comments upon the Danish influence, "gabled and shingled houses, massive and brightly painted buildings, the statues and coats-of-arms".

* The Church is by Hans van Steenwinckel the Younger, completed in 1696; but the spire is later and there is confusion as to whether it is to his design, or that of Lurids de Thurah of *Den Danske Vitruvius*. It appears to me that this must be so, for grafted on to a typical Dutch building the spire shows a decided, if transmuted influence of Borromini.

muddling that there should be another palace called Frederiksberg on the outskirts of the town. It is now an officers' school
and cannot be seen without permission. But it is here we first
come upon the stucco ceilings which are so splendid a feature
of certain Danish palaces and country houses. They are the
work of travelling craftsmen from the Ticino; there being in
all some eighteen of these ceilings at Frederiksberg, half by
Domenico Carbonetti and half by Francesco Quadri, though
only the closest study would reveal the difference between
them. I am bound to say, though, that the present uses of
Frederiksberg, in spite of their excellent state of conservation,
do not make this palace a favourable place in which to
judge of their handiwork, which in other and more congenial
settings is to be reckoned among the prime beauties of
Denmark. Cheap wallpapers, billiard tables, wall maps and
all the paraphernalia of a military college detract from
Frederiksberg where, indeed, the chief interest is the chapel
and the Queen's marble bathroom. But Frederiksberg is
worth a visit, also, for its gardens.

Just as, if you go to Spain during winter you miss the bull
fights, if you are in Copenhagen in August you do not see the
Ballet, and this to a ballet lover is a serious loss. Many and
many a time did I walk from the Kongens Nytorv to the
Royal Theatre examining it in every particular, and looking
regretfully at the old posters. Worse still at the new ones, for
the season was to begin again on 1 September, the day after
we were to leave for home. With the Royal Danish Ballet the
interest is the old ballets of Bournonville. Of French descent,
he was born in Copenhagen in 1805, but went early to study
under Vestris, where he danced with Marie Taglioni and with
Fanny Elssler. Returning to Copenhagen Bournonville worked
there for a quarter of a century at his ballets, some dozen of
which are still in the repertory, then worked abroad again,
and died in 1879. What I wished most to see was his ballet
Napoli, with scenes in the blue grotto and ending with a
brilliant chain of tarantellas*; his version of the original *La*

* The third act of *Napoli* with its tarantellas was revived for
The Festival Ballet from the original choreography, and given in
London in 1954, and again in 1955. Further information on Bournon-

Sylphide which is still performed; and the recently revived *Kermesse de Bruges* with music by Adolphe Adam; perhaps, also, his *La Fête à Albano* written to celebrate Thorvaldsen's triumphant return from Rome to his native city, with figures and groups based on the sculptor's works. Before leaving Copenhagen we were able, at least to see the dancers in class, but this did not compensate for missing *Napoli*, that living relic of Naples of the Bourbon Kings surviving, so curiously, in the northern capital. The 'school' of Bournonville is perceptible in certain movements to connoisseurs of dancing, and it is among the anomalies of modern times that this hoard of classical ballets should still be performed in Copenhagen when the classical repertory is supposed, generally, to consist of *Giselle* and *Coppélia* and the trio of Tchaikowsky-Petipa works, *Swan Lake, The Sleeping Beauty,* and the shorter, two act *Casse-Noisette. Napoli*, in particular, is a living fossil of the painters of all nationalities who met daily in the Caffè Greco in Rome, and of the Scuola di Posilipo.

But it is time to go again, as I did so often, to the patrician part of Copenhagen, walking down Bredgade towards Amalienborg. This is the quarter called Frederiksstaden laid out under Frederik V (1746–66) to the plans of his architect Nicolai Eigtved, a name to remember in European rococo when, if ever, that word ceases to imply abuse. For it is, in fact, a quarter of most elegant and graceful buildings placing this part of Copenhagen on an equal with the Place Stanislas at Nancy. Several discreet and lovely palaces look out on us from behind iron railings. There is No. 68 Bredgade, built by Eigtved as a hospital, but also Lurids de Thurah had a hand in it, and they are the two big names in Danish eighteenth century architecture. A building of modest size but perfect in proportion, and not anything else but Danish. Near this is the disappointing domed Marble Church, which makes an effect because of its planned and calculated position facing towards Amalienborg but is, aesthetically, only an empty shell. And a few steps away is the nostalgic Russian church of

ville may be found in *Supplement to Complete Book of Ballets* by C. W. Beaumont, London, C. W. Beaumont, 1942, pp. 21–30.

St. Alexander Nevsky, reminding one of other Russian churches in Biarritz and in San Remo and of days when the Grand Dukes sent their laundry to be done in Paris and ordered trainfuls of flowers for their dinner parties from the Riviera. There are other graceful and tall buildings, not all rococo, for some are of Empire date; and then we change our direction, playing a game with ourselves as to which way we shall go into the Amalienborg Square, and walk down the Amaliegade past more old houses and the little modest yellow house, hardly a palace, where our Queen Alexandra was born. Horace Marryat, with his anonymous companion, or companions, had an apartment in the Amaliegade in 1860, and it is surely, still, the quietest and most charming street in Copenhagen.

The Amalienborg Square, we have said before, is diamond-shaped or, at least, it is octagonal, with quadruplet palaces connected by graceful colonnades. Its history is that, as usual, the Royal Palace had been burnt down; and these four palaces built by noble families were taken over by the King.* Since 1794 it has been the Royal Palace. The King lives in one of them, has his State apartment in another, and the other pair of palaces (those furthest from the harbour) are used by government departments. In the middle of the square is the equestrian statue of Frederik V by the Frenchman J. F. J. Saly, made and cast by order of the East Asiatic Company in 1771. The statue is not nearly so fine and imposing as the majestic *haute école* figure of Dom José I at Lisbon, advancing in plumed helm on his long tailed circus horse across the square towards the blue waters of the Tagus. But the buildings of that square are meaningless. Here, they are graceful and delightful and intimate, and it is perhaps because of that character that it is better they should face inwards, away from the harbour and towards the town. Also, the very octagonal, or diamond, shape of the enclosed space makes it that the eye is contained in the square of Amalienborg, looking from one palace to the other. It is

* The palace containing the State Rooms was built by Count Moltke; the others were built by Count Schack, Baron Brockdorff, and Count Levetzau.

almost, indeed, more of an architectural interior, an interior square, not a perspective or a panorama, and this planning is, decidedly, more suited to the climate of Denmark, which is not that of the Bosphorus or the Bay of Naples. It is ideally suited to the northern light and to the Baltic, the shipping of which is but a few yards away; and you are aware of that but are not blown round corners in and out of the square by sea winds, here, where all is symmetry and order.

To the tens of thousands of spectators who have watched the Changing of the Guard in the Amalienborg Square, year after year, part of the pleasure of the spectacle derives from this harmony and balance in the architecture. It is, in essence, the same delight as that of the small boy seeing the engine go under bridges and through tunnels on a toy railway, while always returning punctually to its starting point. The route leads from the barracks of the Danish Life Guard in the Rosenborg Gardens, and traverses so many streets with houses and palaces dating from the eighteenth and nineteenth centuries which were the age of order. In terms of London we would have to agree that the Regency architecture of Carlton House Terrace and even the low lines of Wellington Barracks give a better background for military spectacles than Buckingham Palace, the front of which is lacking in character and architecturally meaningless. The Changing of the Guard in the court of St. James's Palace is another matter altogether because the buildings are in scale, and also the dark colour of the brick enhances the red coats. The Trooping of the Colour gains immeasurably as a spectacle because of the building of the Horse Guards being by so good an architect as William Kent. In order to feel sure of this we have but to imagine the Trooping of the Colour on a parade ground in front of the Victoria and Albert Museum or, worse still, the National History Museum along Cromwell Road. Or, if we like to think of it as taking place in front of Selfridges', then it is to admit that there is little to choose in banality between Selfridges' and Buckingham Palace. But at the Amalienborg in Copenhagen this military spectacle is to be enjoyed in an unrivalled setting which, and this is typical, was not designed especially, the four palaces having been built, as we know, for private owners.

The uniform of the Danish Life Guard must be a little older in invention than that of our Foot Guards. It would appear to date from 1820 to 1830, with the exception of the bearskin which I would think is definitely of earlier origin as it closely resembles those worn in eighteenth century portraits, including one of the Dauphin, son of Louis XV, in the National Gallery in London. Their step is different from that of our Foot Guards, another length of step, I apprehend, and a different pace, and the Danish Life Guard have, as well, that curious way of holding their rifles with both arms folded in front of them. Even when the Royal Family are not in residence there are some six to eight sentries pacing up and down in their undress uniform of dark blue tunics and light blue trousers with a stripe. On more important occasions this is exchanged for pale blue trousers and scarlet red tunic. Their guard room in the building at the right-hand corner of the colonnade opening on Amalie Gade has rifles piled outside it, and is perhaps the best of all angles from which to survey the square. A word of praise must be extended to their sentry boxes, the most effectively designed that one has ever seen, octagonal wooden structures painted in the Royal colour of red, and with the King's number and cypher put in a conspicuous place above the opening. The Changing of the Guard is the pride of Copenhagen, and in a Europe dwindled of Royal bodyguards this is one of the few that are left. Gone are the Hungarian Guard in scarlet hussar uniform enriched with silver lace, tiger-skin pellisse, high yellow boots and high fur cap surmounted with a heron plume, with their grey horses with green housings and silver bridles, and their colonel who on appointment became a baron of the Holy Roman Empire. Gone, too, the Trabant Guard of the Austrian Kaisers, halberdiers in red coats worked with gold lace, and white waistcoat and breeches. Vanished, also, the Chevaliers Gardes and Gardes à Cheval of the Russian Tzars, the Cossacks of the Guard, snub-nosed Pavlovski Guard in high grenadier caps, and all the others. There remain the breast plated Household Cavalry of England, the Brigade of

Guards, and, if you like, the Yeomen of the Guard. And the
Swiss Guard of the Popes'; and that is all. Excepting for the
Danish Life Guard, and their other *corps d'élite*, the Royal
Hussars, not often seen now in the capital, for they are
quartered at Nastved a country town in the middle of
Zealand, but at balls and Court ceremonies in the Amalienborg they still enliven the scene in their full dress uniform of
pale blue and a red dolman edged with astrakhan, with a
silver stripe. At about the time when the Kings of Denmark
were giving the albino horses with pink eyes and ears to
draw the Tsarina's carriage there was close contact between
this Royal Hussar Regiment and the Russian Imperial
Court. The Tsar Alexander III, brother-in-law of our Queen
Alexandra, was made Colonel-in-Chief of the regiment. A
fine portrait of the giant Tsar by Valentin Serov, wearing the
red dress uniform with Fredensborg Castle in the background, was presented to the regiment and hangs in their
mess.*

But it is time to turn our attention to the interiors of the
four palaces of the Amalienborg. That one of the four used by
the King for State ceremonies is, like the others, by Nicolai
Eigtved, one of the two good architects of the Danish
eighteenth century. It is not open to the public but is seen at

* Lent by the Royal Life Guards, Copenhagen, to the Exhibition of
Russian Art at No. 1, Belgrave Square in 1953. Another relic of
similar association must be Tchaikowsky's *Festival Overture on the
Danish National Hymn*, his Opus 15, composed in 1866 to celebrate the
marriage of the Tsarevitch (Alexander III) with Princess Dagmar
(sister of Queen Alexandra). "Of all his early works, this is the only
one which he himself judged favourably in his later years. . . . In
regard to this Overture he wrote only a year or two before his death
that he considered it not only effective, but musically superior to the
well known *1812*." (This is quoted from *Tchaikowsky*, by Edwin
Evans, London, J. M. Dent & Sons, *The Master Musicians Series*,
1935, pp. 20, 138, 139.) The Danish National Hymn dates from 1780,
and it is perhaps a serious omission that this work of Tchaikowsky's,
so far as the writer knows, is now never performed. Before we leave
this subject it is perhaps worth noting that the *Almanach de Gotha* of
1857 gives two squadrons of Gardes du Corps à Cheval in addition to
the Royal Hussars, but these seem to have disappeared in the course
of time.

State receptions and banquets to members of the diplomatic corps, and contains fine French furniture, Royal portraits, and good stucco ceilings*, but it may be that a little and peculiar interest attaches because of the heyducks. These were, originally, running footmen put into Hungarian or Polish dress. There are, for instance, heyducks in Bernardo Bellotto's paintings of Dresden and of Warsaw, 'heyduck', like 'hussar', being a word of Hungarian connotation. There were heyducks attached to the service of the Empress Maria-Theresa and to the Empress Catherine the Great. They persisted at the court of the Tsars in the form of *Skorokhods* or running footmen, until the Revolution, but now are extinct everywhere save at the Amalienborg, where there are still heyducks, but of a special kind.

One of the most picturesque of all State ceremonies must be that upon the King's birthday when a reception is given and the stair of the palace is lined with heyducks wearing pots of artificial flowers in their half-mitre or grenadier caps. Long ago I was told of this ceremony, of which I have never to date been able to find a painting or even a drawing, except a little vignette, an inch high, of one of the hats drawn in the margin of a book by an Englishman passing through Copenhagen on his way to the Coronation of Nicholas II in Moscow in 1893; and the drawing, already described, to be seen on the programme of a gala performance of the Royal Ballet, this latter in the Rosenborg Castle. Nothing seems to be known of the origin of this extraordinary headgear which could very well be an invention from a fairy story. A foreign diplomat, newly arrived at the Danish Court, has told me of his astonished interest at seeing one of the heyducks standing at the banquet behind the Queen's chair. I do not know how many of the old uniforms are in existence, but they must be in considerable number if there are enough to line the stair, It is, therefore, with great pleasure that we are permitted here to reproduce a photograph specially taken by the Court photographer, probably the first ever taken, of one of the heyducks in his flower-pot

* The interiors of the Amalienborg are the subject of a monograph, *Amalienborg-Interiører*, by Christian Elling, Copenhagen, 1945.

hat. It will be seen that the front of the cap is that of a grenadier's half-mitre hat, as worn by the grenadiers of Frederick the Great, and that the rest of the hat appears to be of red velvet and gold lace, with the false nosegay inserted into the crown. The coat is, of course, of the Royal red; there is a gold sash, and white breeches. It is only a pity that the heyducks in their unique uniforms are not seen except by those privileged few who have access to the interior of the Amalienborg, for certainly with the Tivoli Gardens and the Danish Life Guard they are among things that are special and peculiar to the Danish capital. Or in this age of universal publicity is it not better that there is something in this quadrumvirate of beautiful palaces, something from the eighteenth century that is kept inviolate and unknown?

At night in Copenhagen, as always, the attraction is the Tivoli Gardens. And this although on four out of every five evenings during August 1954 it entailed standing, or running, in the rain. But rain does not matter when it is a question of Italian pantomime. The open air theatre is just by the main entrance, and every evening there is a large crowd waiting for the huge peacock of the drop curtain to fold down its tail. A theatre which is a *chinoiserie* pavilion and has, as one writer says of it, "nothing whatever to do with China proper, but is as we imagine China to be". In fact, it is in the *chinoiserie* of the tea-canister and of some of the more jejune parts of Brighton Pavilion, but all the better for that.* Ballets are performed here, also, but above all it is the Italian pantomime, or harlequinade, lasting only for some twenty minutes, but taking you with it into a world of pure enchantment.

The repertory consists, I believe, of some twenty or thirty pantomimes, of which four or five are given every summer. They contain any number of old tricks, many of them coming straight down from the time of the Italian comedians whom

* Or, as my brother writes in his preface to *Escape with Me*, "I shall continue to call it Peking, and neither Pekin nor the modern Peiping, for it is as Peking that I have always thought of it since I first read its magic name in childhood upon the programme of a pantomime." *Escape with Me*, by Osbert Sitwell, London, Macmillan & Co., 1939, pp. ix–x.

Watteau painted. The *dramatis personae* is still that, entirely, of the *Commedia dell'Arte*, with one or two additional characters and a Danish flavouring. Pierrot, for one, has been entirely altered and is scarcely to be recognised from the melancholy waif known to the English audiences from uninspired performances of Schumann's *Carnaval*. This is due to Niels Hendrik Volkersen, the great Pierrot of the Tivoli Gardens who played the part for nearly fifty years, and of whom there is the excellent statue near the theatre, his head and shoulders on a pedestal and a medallion of him from life, below. The present Pierrot is, so to speak, his understudy, wearing the same 'make up' and, no doubt, largely copying him in temperament. The Pierrot of Tivoli Gardens is old and kind and genial, restorer of lost situations, and the character who puts things to right again, beloved especially, therefore, by the children in his audience*.

There are street scenes in the old Italian tradition; comic peasants unloading handcarts, these in their flaxen wigs resembling Kändler's Meissen Harlequins; valets in knee-breeches; interiors like rooms from *Don Pasquale* or *The Barber of Seville*; and, of course, Harlequin and Columbine. Pierrot puts to sea in a barrel, or sometimes agrees to have himself locked up and corded in a trunk. It is always worth a journey in order to see a spangled Harlequin, and there are beautiful and unforgettable moments as when Harlequin leaps onto the stool where Columbine in her short skirt sits before her looking-glass, they look into it together for a held moment, and he leaps down and runs off stage. On a particular night this scene looked more beautiful than before seen in the spangled rain. It will always remind one that Watteau painted Harlequin, that he was a subject for Cézanne, and has been painted and drawn so often by Picasso that Harlequins have become almost a part of the signature or sign manual of that protean genius of our age and time. On various evenings I watched two Columbines, and was told that one of them, most graceful with her Nordic colouring and

* The Pierrot of the Tivoli Theatre more resembles the *Gilles* of Watteau's painting in the Louvre, but Gilles is no longer youthful but middle-aged.

64

fair hair, married to Harlequin, would soon go back with him
to Iceland to found a national ballet there which does, indeed,
seem a long way to have come from Bergamo!

Tivoli is one of those ideal places the geography of which
never becomes quite settled in one's mind. And how much
better so! For it is, of course, not really very large in area,
and is right in the middle of the town. In the background,
always delighted shrieks from the fun fair and the blare of
the steam-organ, but it is probably, by now, electrical or oil-
driven, and penny gambling hells where no one can be ruined.
Concert halls, enclosed and open air; and the statue to Gade
the waltz composer of the Tivoli Gardens, violin on shoulder,
"sawing away, regardless", as Sir Henry Wood would have
said, and surrounded by dancing babies some few of whom
with his every movement it would be impossible for him not
to kick and maim. There are lakes, bridges, fountains,
kiosques and, of course, fairy lights. And two or three excellent restaurants besides *La Belle Terrasse*; *Divan I* and *Divan
II*, in particular, run by two brothers, and perhaps more
especially the second. It was to *Divan II* we used to come
running evening after evening through the rain. Or was it
Divan I? There is, also, *Tårnpavillonen*; but *Divans I* and *II*
are particularly delightful, with their white trelliswork,
tables at different levels, and menus more like a guide to a
celestial picture gallery than a mere list of dishes marked with
prices.

During the course of the month we spent in Copenhagen
we left the capital again and again on journeys to the islands,
and on each and every occasion it is Rosenborg, the Amalienborg, and Tivoli that one misses, and is glad to return to.
Copenhagen must be, these and other things considered, the
lightest and gayest city in Northern Europe, perhaps of all
Europe after Rome and Paris. Why, for instance, Edinburgh
cannot vie with it is one of those mysteries of nationality which
it is almost impossible to explain. But it is by the same token
that Hamburg, not so many miles away, is heavy, heavy,
however frenzied its attempts at gaiety, and that no powers
in earth or heaven could 'put on' the Feria of Seville in
Glasgow or in Aberdeen. Yet the gaiety of Copenhagen, all

said and done, does not amount to much. It is only that there is lightness and sparkle in the air; that the Danes are much less heavy than Swedes or Norwegians and, individually, like sunmotes or flakes of snow in comparison to Germans, everywhere. And that it is a town of fine eighteenth century architecture, good modern buildings, and light in the hand, delightful Danes.

21 COPENHAGEN. The Amalienborg Palaces (1760. *Nicolai Eigtved, architect*) and the Equestrian Statue of Frederik V (1771. *J. F. J. Saly, sculptor*)

CHAPTER III

Zealand, its Landscapes and its Castles

ROM Copenhagen sooner or later, whether you like it or not, you will find yourself on the way to Elsinore. To the Danes it is a mixture of the Tower of London, Stratford-on-Avon, and Windsor Castle—all three of them together and less than an hour away. And, in fact, it is a nice drive with Sweden coming nearer in sight along the Sound. Practically, a long line of summer villas with myriads of little yachts flaunting their white sails. Soon, a town the other side of the water looms and comes nearer, and is Helsingborg in Sweden only a few minutes away. It is like looking from Algeciras to whitewashed Ceuta only a mile or two in the distance, but across the Straits of Gibraltar and in Africa; Sweden might be another continent, except that there are no fig trees or cactuses, and that it is not like Africa at all. And now we are in Elsinore, which the Danes call Helsingør, with its few old houses, and go along by the harbour to the Castle of Kronborg. Here, there is a good deal of bother and long distances to go, but at last we come to the swans upon the moat, the copper spires of the Castle, and the ramparts where Hamlet walked.

There is a fine Renaissance courtyard where *Hamlet* is performed, and the great Hall of the Knights with stone floor, red-beamed ceiling, and tapestries upon the walls. But Kronborg Castle was for too long a barracks, until 1922; though it is superb in situation guarding the entrance to the Sound, more than for content which, in fact, amounts to little if anything at all. Maybe it was better when it was a barracks, while the bugles still announced the ghosts, for

Hamlet and his father are not the only ones to haunt the Castle. Queen Carolina Matilda, sister of our George III, was imprisoned in two little rooms here after her lover Struensee had been beheaded. Kronborg Castle must have been at its most marvellous about a hundred years ago when Horace Marryat was able to take rooms in the nearby palace of Marienlyst*, "with two large white glazed busts of Christian VI and his son Frederik V in all the glory of elephants and periwigs upon the stair", where, too, the *front fuyant* dawned upon him, so remarkable, as he says, "among all monarchs from the commencement of the eighteenth century, for the forehead recedes giving an *air moutonnier*", and he concludes that it is not "that the nurses of that century indulged in some bandaging or manipulation of the infant head like that which exists among certain Red Indian tribes, but that it can only be attributed to the weight of the pigtails attached to the wigs by which their youthful heads were disfigured".

About half an hour away through the lonely beechwoods is swan-white Fredensborg. The phrase is Marryat's, and well describes it, or at least the impression that the palace gives, for unfortunately the Royal Family were in residence and we could not go inside. Beautiful old lime avenues lead to it, and there are statues, clipped hedges†, mirroring waters. I would

* As when Washington Irving took up his quarters and encamped in the Alhambra. One of the most romantic of all ruins, even in Spain, is that of the cathedral at Lerida, in Catalonia, still a cavalry barracks. We were shown round four years ago by a half-witted conscript. Till lately, and perhaps even now, the nave was used for machine gun instruction, the aisles were dormitories, and the cloisters contained the kitchens and canteen. Lerida cathedral would be a hundred times more beautiful as a church, of course, but better as it is, than as a dead museum with postcard stalls and ticket sellers. At least, its ghosts are kept alive by bugle calls.

† The Norwegian 'amphitheatre' with sixty-nine sandstone figures of peasants and fishermen from Norway, then ruled by Denmark, Iceland, and the Faroe Islands, lies at the back and looks to be not very interesting. But, also, according to Marryat, there are many small statues "of no particular excellence" by Charles Stanley, who made the monument of Queen Louisa, daughter of our George II, in the cathedral of Roskilde. This Anglo-Dane sculptor spent twenty years of his life in England (1726–46), and works are ascribed to him at

like to have seen the interior of Fredensborg if only for
its portraits, particularly that mentioned by Marryat of
Frederik IV, builder of the palace, and for its fine ceilings of
which the same writer remarks, wisely, and so much out of
his time, "I like a fine suite of rooms, richly moulded and
painted ceilings, and in all the buildings of Frederik IV you
have these to perfection. I never saw his plasterwork surpassed in any country." If the stucco ceilings of Fredensborg
be as splendid as those of distant Clausholm, then they are
magnificent indeed. And we came away reluctantly from
'swan-white' Fredensborg, looking back at it down the
avenue, well believing how Queen Alexandra may have loved
it when there were the summer parties there with her sister
the Gospodina and the giant, good natured Tsar, and she
could eat her favourite Danish dish of rødgrød, a sort of cold
soup of red currants eaten with sugar and whey. And looking
back for the last time there was a solitary sentry of the Danish
Life Guard pacing up and down, and one could see his bearskin and clasped rifle and his cat-like walk down the avenue
against the 'swan-white' wall.

The Danish beechwoods now begin in all their beauty with
blue lakes between, and of another character altogether
from, say, the Buckinghamshire beechwoods which are in the
nature of hanging woods and groves. These are at dead level;
the ground hardly rises at all, and again they are entirely
different, as we shall see, from the beechwoods of Sweden,
which are more northern still. Round Fredensborg there are
many miles of beechwoods, and cornfields, too, and in the
middle of it all the town of Hillerød, which *is* Frederiksborg
Castle; and here again it is muddling, for Fredensborg has
nothing to do with a name, it only means the Castle of Peace
or Friendship, whereas Frederiksborg *is* called after Frederik
but was built by Christian IV. Two Dutchmen, the brothers

Compton Palace, Eastbourne; Langley Park, Norfolk; Honington
Hall, Warwickshire; and above all the ceiling panel of *Venus and
Adonis*, influenced by Titian's painting, at Easton Neston, North-
amptonshire; perhaps, also, at Stoneleigh Abbey, Warwickshire. His
activities on return to Denmark have not yet been completely ascer-
tained.

71

Steenwinckel, were his architects and, baldly, it is built upon three islets in a lake. All in Dutch style, of red brick with sandstone dressings, all spires and gables, golden balls and gilded finials, with on that sunny morning a stork that perched obligingly on a crocket, but nearly blinding you to look at it. A bigger, taller, redder, more northern Hampton Court, with nothing Italian about it; and at last, crossing the moat and over the cobble stones, there is the great Neptune fountain of Adriaen de Vries in the courtyard, but it is, in fact, a copy.* It now begins to dawn upon one, if one has not thought of if before, that the Castle of Frederiksborg is tremendously restored, and, of course, the truth is that it was burnt out after one of the usual fires in Royal palaces in Denmark. This particular, fatal incident was in 1859, and the signature of that time is written heavily in restoration. And yet, the original being of a date that painted and gilded with a heavy hand, it is perhaps not so entire a travesty of what was before. All things considered, the seventeenth century in Northern Europe was *not* one of those epochs when the hand of man could not go wrong. This may even have been an infection that emanated from Northern Italy, for we have to take into account the bad taste of the Certosa di Pavia and the intricate ugliness of much work from armour to marquetry that had its origin in Milan. The same criticism applies to many of the French châteaux and to furniture made under the Valois Kings and in the time of Henri IV. It could be said equally of the Castle at Heidelberg, that 'jewel' of the German Renaissance, and of masterworks of Dutch architecture, so called, such as Lieven de Key's Meat Market at Haarlem; while, in England, houses as beautiful (and that in the highest, most poetical meaning) as Hardwick, as Montacute, or as Kirby Hall, have to be put in the balance against Wollaton, Hatfield, Burleigh, and other achievements of heavier hands and eyes. What we

* The original Neptune fountain by Adriaen de Vries was removed to Sweden by Charles X in 1659 as spoils of war, and now stands in the garden of Drottningholm, outside Stockholm. Adriaen de Vries was perhaps the greatest of the non-Italian baroque sculptors of Northern Europe. Born at The Hague c. 1550 he died in Prague in 1626.

would call, generally, buildings of the Elizabethan or Jacobean period are adventurous but uncertain in touch, and just because of their date they are not, *ipso facto*, masterpieces of the highest art. But, in the long list of such castles and other buildings, it is true to say that Frederiksborg, despite restoration, remains long in mind.

It is because of the strong personality of Christian IV, its builder. This is at its most potent in the Castle Chapel; pews or closets for the King and his family, of ebony and inlaid woods; pulpit and high altar and organ case, intricately carved and gilded; and ceiling of ebony with pendant ornaments of ivory, many of them turned by King Christian in his workshop. Also, the shields of the Knights of the Elephant, for this is the chapel of that Order of Chivalry, as is the Garter Chapel at St. George's, Windsor, to Knights of the Garter.* Above, up a winding stair, is the Riddersaal, where the King dined after the great hunting parties with his friends. But the interest of Frederiksborg is, really, its collection of historical portraits. There is room after room of these, and every room is interesting. And here for the first time we meet the widows of Denmark, sixteenth and seventeenth century ladies of astonishing sourness of countenance, and something peculiar to Denmark, for in no other country do you see their like. But the guide to these Royal portraits is Horace Marryat, who made a special study of them. Among the earliest (before 1500) he mentioned that of an early Queen, wife of the first of the Oldenburg Kings, wearing on her head "a strange headdress formed of linen, with a sort of gag of

---

* In the church at Boxted in Suffolk, near Long Melford, there is the standing statue of a knight in armour with a little golden frog hanging from his right ear. This is Sir John Poley, who fought under Elizabeth and James I, and also under Henri IV of France. He was made a Knight of the Elephant, and his frog-earring is said to be among the emblems of that Order, its import being perhaps that the frog and the elephant are, respectively, the biggest and the smallest quadrupeds known in nature. No one in Denmark has heard of this, or seems able to offer any explanation, but the Order of the Elephant was reconstituted and dates, in its modern form, from the reign of Christian V (1670–99), nearly a hundred years later than the statue to Sir John Poley.

73

the same material across her mouth, such as is still worn by the peasant women of the island of Laesø, as well as in parts of Jutland, as a preservative against the injury caused to their lungs by the flying sand". He tells, also, of the portrait of Adolf, first of the line of Holstein-Gottorp (1526–86) and says of him that "no one who regards his portrait and his son's sons, from generation to generation, can doubt for the moment from whom the late Tsar Nicholas I of Russia derived his almost demi-god-like beauty".* There are portraits, of course, of the great Christian, including a remarkable one of him in his grave clothes lying on his deathbed, and of some at least of his twenty-two children, all told, "the race of Gyldenløves, sons of the Karens, the Vibekes, and the other Ladies of Rosenborg". The best of the portraits being by the Dutchman Abraham Wuchters, and in nearly every one that depicts a lady contemporary to Christian IV there is one of the curious breed of dogs, half-bulldog, half-mastiff, bred by the King and given to his friends.†

But alas! many, if not most, of the earlier portraits perished in the fire of 1859, an account of which is to be found in Marryat's postscript to his second volume under date 17 December, and there is so true a touch of poetry in it than

* The classical profile of this Tsar, grandson of Catherine the Great, is still to be recaptured from the cameo-like engraving of him upon bottles of Mentzendorff Kümmel. His good looks, it could be said, descend directly in a living instance, through her mother the Russian Grand Duchess Helena, to the Duchess of Kent and Princess Alexandra.

† Karel van Mander (b. Courtrai, 1579) went to Denmark, where he painted portraits and designed tapestries for Christian IV. His son, of the same name, went on his father's death on 1623 to Copenhagen, and was appointed Court painter. He died in Holland. Abraham Wuchters, another Dutchman, went with Karel van Mander the Younger, his brother-in-law, to Denmark in 1638, and remained there till his death in 1683, painting, it is said, over fifty portraits of the King, his family, and other persons of rank. These are the three seventeenth century portrait painters most commonly met with in collections in Denmark. Abraham Wuchters is a generation later in date than Cornelius Janssen or Paul van Somers, Dutch painters who worked in England in the reign of James I, but he offers the same costume interest and is fascinating in a minor key because of the strange Northern types whom he portrayed.

one cannot forbear to quote. He was sitting in his room at
the hotel in Elsinore, "busily and happily immersed in his
books", when the chambermaid burst into his room to tell
him that the castle was on fire. In three-quarters of an hour
he was on his way "as fast as post-horses and a highly-
booted postilion could carry him", arriving in time to see the
burning castle and the Royal portraits being carried out into
the snow. The earlier ones were gone. "Do not imagine I slept
that night: no—I lay tossing on my bed; the spectre of that
gallery was for ever before my eyes. Good Queen Sophia with
her pale blue eyes; Christian IV with his marlok, and frail
Christina Munk; the splendid family of Gyldenløves; Adolf
of Holstein, garter on knee, and his giant race", etc., etc.
The next day he returned again to Frederiksborg. "I felt at
once the whole of the earlier portraits of the house of
Oldenburg were doomed. Of that splendid series of two
hundred years and upwards, from Christian I downwards, not
one remained—portraits by Lukas Cranach, by John of
Cleves, Carl van Mander, Wuchters, Jacob van Dort"; all
had gone. And he tells of a portrait of Anne of Denmark,
sister of King Christian and mother of our Charles I, "in
starched ruff and monstrous farthingale, on which sits perched
a small black terrier dog. She wears a red powdered wig, and
on a ribbon in the sky is written her motto: '*La Mia
Grandezza Viene Dal Eccelso*'" (a motto which was surely not
without a fatal influence upon her son!); "and her sister
Augusta of Holstein-Gottorp, with a spotted carriage dog
(Dalmatian) couched at her feet, the only proof we now
possess of these dogs being of this origin." Another portrait
of Anne of Denmark, " in a white dress with a feathered fan
in hand and a flaxen wig, this time almost albino, standing
outrageous in the extravagances of her farthingale ", is enough
to make one wonder why no one has ever undertaken a study
of the extraordinary dresses worn by this Queen, not less far
fetched than those of her predecessor Queen Elizabeth, and
among wearers and instigators of the crinoline every bit as
extreme as the hooped skirts worn by Marie-Antoinette or
the Empress Eugénie. At Hampton Court Palace there is the
curious portrait of Anne of Denmark by Paul van Somer, in

which she is to be seen in hunting dress, in a green riding habit and a plumed hat, standing by a horse of palomino breed with golden coat and silvery mane that her negro groom holds for her, while in her hand are the strings of a *harde* of whippets or Italian greyhounds, each with its name worked on its collar. Portraits of Anne of Denmark from all sources would add up to a curious picture of an age gone by.

In spite of the fire there are at Frederiksborg portraits beyond number of the seventeenth century, including some few which are very curious of persons with exaggeratedly fair hair, and this hair frizzed out to fantastic proportions as though they were making play of being Danes, though nothing so far fetched after this manner as the family group at Gaunø, of an immense number of brothers and sisters all distinguished in this fashion. Later centuries at Frederiksborg are no less interesting. And here we have the truly extraordinary painting of Frederik IV by Benoit Coffre, a Frenchman who was at work as well on painted ceilings in the castle. It would not be untrue to say that this is one of the most peculiar of all Royal portraits. With his feet in the first position in dancing as though about to start upon a gavotte or minuet, the King wears armour, balances his sceptre at an angle in one hand, and with other arm akimbo affectedly sweeps his ermine robe which must have been of prodigious weight around him. But most strange of all is the face within the periwig, and this is the King who while married to Louise of Mecklenburgh met Anna Reventlow, daughter of his Grand Chancellor, at a masquerade (of which masked ball he later had a painted ceiling made at Frederiksborg by this same obliging artist), drove up by night to Clausholm to a side door, and eloped with her, contracted a 'conscience marriage' with her, creating her Countess of Sleswig, and for ten years "lived with her, the husband of two wives, until the death of his first queen", when he married her a few days later. His periwig in the portrait is of huge size, and he appears to move his head and look round in it; his long nose, a narrow chin, and somewhat Habsburg lower lip being of the type which prevailed so strongly in the Oldenburg family, and

23   King Frederik IV (1699–1730)

From the portrait by Benoit Coffre

25 Queen Louise (1724–57)

24 Queen Juliane Marie (1729–96)

which in the words of my Danish informant* "is recognizable in almost all Danish Kings from the accession to the throne of the first member of the House of Oldenburg in 1448 until the extinguishing of their line in 1863". What a strange little King without his periwig! In the background of the portrait are a triumphal column, a garden, and the corner of a palace, the whole effect I have said, being that of King Florestan in the fairy story, and the palace of the Sleeping Beauty being the castle of Clausholm where we are to meet again, eventually, far away in Jutland.

Other portraits from the eighteenth century here are little less excessive, in particular, members of the Augustenborg family. In the days of ill defined frontiers they ruled a little principality of their own, now in Denmark, now within the German Diet, being, as it were, cousins in perpetuity to the Danish Kings. In them *le front fuyant* is seen at its most extreme of sloping, and some of their countenances are scarcely to be credited, more fantastic still because of their minor history which is almost impossible to unravel. More portraits, too, of Frederik VI, that late anachronism in appearance (he only died in 1839), but characterized by Marryat as "the best King that had reigned, to date, in Denmark", his strange features being made but more interesting when the same writer, speaking of a portrait of Queen Sophia Amelia of Brunswick, wife of Frederik III (d. 1670), tells us that "it was from her the present Royal family of Denmark inherit the projecting chin and under jaw which characterize the House of Oldenburg".

It is with a mind haunted by many ghosts that one comes back from Frederiksborg, and all the more haunting because one had heard of so few of them before. But the next project after visiting the Royal castles was to see the lay convents in Denmark, and this was more difficult of execution. Marryat refers delightfully to them, and there are the engravings in Lurids de Thurah's *Den Danske Vitruvius*. We had had a little foretaste in visiting the lay convent at Roskilde, but now we wished to see Vallø, and Gisselfeld, and Vemmetofte, and this

* Mr. H. A. Holck Colding, who has given me his kind assistance in many points of this book.

called for preparation and for time since one had to ask for permission or get introductions. Having for long heard of these lay convents I was most anxious to go inside them.

Gisselfeld, the first we visited, is the property of the Danneskjold-Samsø family, and their eldest unmarried daughter becomes the Abbess. It came into possession of one of the two Gyldenløves, son of Christian V. He served in Italy under Prince Eugéne commanding the Italian troops, but died young, and by his will bequeathed the manor of Gisselfeld to found a convent for noble ladies. So far Marryat, who after telling us about that family connection continues, gaily, "As for the nuns, they are flitting about the world somewhere."

We left Copenhagen on a wet leaden morning in company with our friend Countess Helle Danneskjold, lately appointed Abbess, or I prefer it, Prioress, by her cousin, it being the sort of wet morning that is habitual in Holland, that is always in force whatever the time of year if you are going to Haarlem, to Delft, or to Leyden, and that explains the grey skies in paintings by Ruysdael or van Goyen. But the weather in Denmark is either more willing or has more powers of recuperation, the road led southwards along the shore of the Sound, and presently the sun came out and the pale cornfields were once again the colour of the Danish children's hair. To the left, as we came along, we could see the spires of Vallø above the distant beechwoods, making me think of so many nunneries and monasteries I have seen, to which the lay convents of Denmark form so curious a supplement or appendix. Gisselfeld is down in the south of Zealand about forty miles from Copenhagen, and like its sisters has the curious habit, which Marryat notices, of hiding itself away. "Gisselfeld", he writes, "was always somewhere, never where we expected it, till I almost fancied it to be a *plaisanterie* of our friend, the Fata Morgana. At last, after turning off into a sort of park, mushroom bedecked and richly timbered . . . we turn into the gardens of the abbey. Nature has here done much, for she undulates well and supplies a lake of water; the slopes are clad with emerald turf and ornamental shrubs, *sorbi* and *crataegi*, in all the glory of their golden and blood-red autumn flowers, and the garden is well backed with beechen woods. Gisselfeld, of course, disappears from the scene, and we were some time before we found the entrance to the fine outbuilding. One of Denmark's best", he concludes, "but whitewashed", which it is no longer, being a red brick building of the middle of the century, of typical gaard or Danish castle form, that is to say, moated, and with stepped gables, having begun life as a castle of the Oxe family, one of whom was uncle to the famous Tycho Brahe, before it became a lay convent.

Crossing the moat we entered the convent, and found ourselves in the long passage of this beautiful old house where the cousin of our friend the Prioress, and proprietor of Gisselfeld, was waiting to receive us. Above the fireplace in one of the downstair rooms hangs an equestrian portrait with a curious history. It is by the Huguenot painter, Jacques d'Agard, who leaving France at the time of the Revocation of the Edict of Nantes was invited to the Court of Denmark, where he was greatly patronized by Christian V, father of the Gyldenløve who founded Gisselfeld.* This is nothing other than the equestrian portrait of our Charles II, said to have been formerly in the gallery at Christiansborg, the head having been altered by d'Agard into a portrait of the Gyldenløve, Proceeding upstairs, we had luncheon in a room with views in every direction over the lakes and park. A feature of Gisselfeld is the extraordinary display of china. Fine services of Meissen, Copenhagen, and other wares are arranged in many of the rooms and all along the passages. Never, out of a museum, has one seen such a quantity of china, and its arrangement must still be that of a hundred or more years ago. One remembers Gisselfeld because of this inordinate amount of china, and for its lakes and trees. The atmosphere is that of a beautiful old country house with good shooting in the woods, and

---

* Jacques d'Agard came to England, according to Horace Walpole, and painted the portraits of many eminent persons of Queen Anne's reign, including the Duchess of Montagu, the Countesses of Rochfort and Sunderland, Thomas, Earl of Strafford, and others. His self-portrait, painted by order of Christian V, hangs in the Uffizi. He died in 1716 at Copenhagen. Little or nothing seems to be known of the portraits that he painted while in England.

the planting is at its best because the stands of beech trees must be a hundred and a hundred and fifty years old, all laid out and dug and planted by some landscape architect who had surely looked at woods and lakes in England.

But some little thing was missing, and before luncheon I had found it in one of the smaller rooms. Having been of opinion from the moment I first heard of them that there must exist some special or peculiar, tangible relics of these unique institutions I had been on the look-out since arriving in Denmark for portraits of the Prioresses, and had noticed one at Frederiksborg. A lady in a pink or *bois de rose* dress, pastoral staff or crozier in hand, wearing the sash of the Order, powdered hair, a delightful cravat, and magnificent earrings of three drops of diamonds. This is Princess Louise Sophie Frederikke of Sleswig-Holsten-Sønderborg-Glucksburg (1709–82), Prioress of Vallø, and the decoration that she wears on the sash across her bosom, I am informed, is that of *l'Union Parfaite*, instituted by Christian VI on 7 August 1732 on the occasion of the eleventh anniversary of his wedding to Queen Sophie Magdalene of Brandenburg-Bayreuth. What delightful, nonsensical nonentities from the non-atomic age! It is a portrait with the quality of a Pietro Longhi, a pastoral Danish addition to the Venetian eighteenth century. And here in a corner of a room at Gisselfeld was a portrait of another Prioress, this time, confusingly, of Niccoline Rosenkrantz (1721–71), Prioress of Vallø. A nice portrait, but what one hoped to find was a portrait of a Prioress who was a beautiful young woman, and eventually, as we shall see, we were lucky enough to find it. That must wait for the moment, but two or three more portraits of Prioresses have come to light, and there must be others. In every instance, but one, they were painted by Andreas Brünnicke, a quite unknown painter who, by reason and in virtue of them, lives in a little and enclosed world of his own.

Queen Sophie Magdalene who built so many palaces in Denmark and played at founding these lay convents was, as we have said, a Princess of Brandenburg-Bayreuth, and it would seem that something of the sort existed, too, in Germany and that they are not, as one imagined, exclusively

Danish. If they are not, they come down, distantly, at many removes, from the Holy Roman Empire. I had been told there were convents of the same kind in Germany, and then remembered Quedlinburg, not far from Haldberstadt, for here there had been an ancient and most curious institution. The castle on a hill above the town was the residence of the Abbesses of Quedlinburg, who were Princesses of the Holy Roman Empire, independent of all spiritual sovereigns save the Pope, having a vote on the Diet, and a seat on the bench of Rhenish Bishops. They were generally members of Royal or noble families. In the castle were good rococo ceilings and portraits of the Lutheran Abbesses. The town itself, many convents and nunneries, and very extensive domains belonged to the Abbess, and she numbered among her vassals many nobles of high rank. At the Reformation the Abbesses adopted the Lutheran faith, lost their feudal sovereignty, and the greatest part of their estates, while the number of nuns was reduced to five. It reads like a feminine counterpart to All Souls' College, Oxford. The right of presentation belonged to the King of Prussia from 1687 to 1803, when the convent was sequestrated. In the church below the hill the Emperor Henry the Fowler and his wife the Empress Matilda, mother of Otto I, lie buried in front of the high altar with many of the Abbesses, but what was most curious to see was a dried up and withered mummy which had been Aurora von Königsmarck (*la Belle Aurore*), Prioress of Quedlinburg, mistress of Augustus the Strong, the Elector of Saxony and King of Poland, mother of the Maréchal de Saxe, and greatgrandmother of George Sand*. Quedlinburg, and other similar survivals from the mediaeval Empire, would seem to be the true origin of the Danish lay convents.

An opportunity to visit Vemmetofte came a few days later.

* Aurora von Königsmarck was Abbess of Quedlinburg from 1704 to 1718. Maurice de Saxe was born at Goslar in 1696. Among anomalies of the Holy Roman Empire it is perhaps worth recalling Osnabrück, an episcopal principality which from 1648 to 1803 was ruled, alternately, by a Catholic Bishop and a lay Protestant who bore the title of Bishop without sharing the ecclesiastical dignity; the Duke of York, son of George III, being made Bishop of Osnabrück when he was two years old.

83

Again it is in the southern part of Zealand, and in the gay words of Marryat "we are all among the nuns to-day". This chapter was the foundation of Prince Charles, son of Frederik IV, and his sister the Princess Hedvige lived here as Prioress until her death. Marryat gives the date of its founding as 1785, which I think must be incorrect*. He mentions Royal portraits, and says, "none are wanting save that of the Reventlow Queen, who seldom appears out of Jutland". But the Reventlow Queen was stepmother, if that is the correct relationship by which to call the 'conscience Queen', to the founder and his sister the Prioress, and it is not likely they would include a portrait of her among their donations to the convent. Marryat tells us of his "lingering over the tapestries and ancient furniture, the queer old gilded stones, the Chinese scent-bottles of Princess Hedvige", and what he means by "queer old gilded stones" I do not know, but he adds that "in a small turret-chamber leading from the great saloon hang the portraits of the ten first-elected ladies of the chapter, attired in black, bearing on their breasts the badge and star of the Order—ten prettier creatures I have seldom seen".

It was delightful to get lost on the way here, and to have to go up hill, down dale, among the magpie villages, all with tall hollyhocks in their little gardens, and a gabled and white-washed church in the middle. But at last we came to straight lines of trees, clipped hedges, and cottages such as you only see in England near the domains of the "great and good". The estate seems to be beautifully managed and kept up, but the brick convent is alas! rebuilt largely. Here we had tea with the Prioress, a lady whose family had been governors or officials in the Danish East Indies, and who most kindly spared us a sternly effective coldcure. We saw the chapel, the passages with their old portraits, the dining hall with its high backed chairs where the ladies dine together at a table laid with old silver, the old embroideries and worked screens, but of the turret-chamber and the ten, pretty, first-elected ladies of the chapter there was no sign.

* The authentic history of Vemmetofte is that it was founded by Queen Charlotte Amalie, widow of Christian V, in 1735.

Lastly, and again after a few days' interval, to Vallø, "the Queen of all Danish convents", but knowing that it had been burnt down in 1893 with much devastation; and not wishing to inflict ourselves upon the Prioress, who had most kindly offered to see us, we forbore to go inside. Vallø was founded on 28 November 1737 by Queen Sophie Magdalene for an Abbess of Royal or princely birth, a Deaconess descended from counts, and twelve Stifts-Froichens with sixteen quarterings, three of whom had to be ladies-in-waiting. The habit was black; except on special occasions when a white silk dress— that of the Abbess of damask, of the Deaconess of satin, of the Froichens of *gros de tour*—ornamented with black lace was worn and with it a long veil and a turquoise blue mantle, the Abbess's lined with ermine, the Deaconess's with satin, the Froichens with 'taffent'. The Counts Moltke are proprietors or intendants of the convent; and on application to authority a child has her name inscribed upon the books, makes a payment, and from that time receives an annual sum. "Of the Dames de Vallø", Marryat tells us, "whom we see dancing and waltzing about the world in white tarlatan, with grand cordon and badge of the order, most of them receive from sixty to seventy pounds, then later as they get old and high on the list, from one hundred and twenty to one hundred and thirty pounds yearly. The Prioress receives an income of about six hundred pounds." This was in 1860; and we are informed that in 1932 some three hundred ladies of noble birth were receiving annuities, and that there were eleven residents of the Abbey, each occupying a suite of half a dozen rooms. Our friend the Prioress of Vemmetofte told us that she received an annual sum about sufficient to buy herself a new dress (but not in Paris!), and the right to wear the jewel of the Order. The lay convents and Vallø, in particular, are the owners of great estates the whole income of which is really devoted to charitable purposes.

But we must hear what more Marryat has to tell us of the Dames de Vallø. "The ten sisters highest on the list have apartments assigned to them in the convent; they have, of course, their own private rooms; but the drawing-rooms are lighted up of an evening, and they dine together, enjoy their own parson, own doctor, own equipages; a beautiful garden, with greenhouses and a deer park. . . . They hold high rank in the tables of precedence, coming after countesses, and before the wives of count's eldest sons." And he writes of the chapel, "where the ladies say their prayers in a sort of peeresses' pew with the retainers of the establishment, a second pew under the pulpit being set apart for the deaf ones" so that they can hear the sermon.

Of course, having missed the chance of doing so, I now wish I had seen the interior of Vallø. The park and woods are magnificent, as fine as any park in England, and indeed maintained after a fashion that is now impossible in our country. Beautiful old avenues lead towards the convent, and the woods lie in every direction with long drives through them. There is a moat round it, and low lying gardens in the highest state of cultivation, with what would seem to be peach or grape houses. Altogether, the woods of Vallø make of it one of the beauties of Denmark, as much so as the beech-woods round Fredensborg. In the interior there are, at least, a few things saved from the fire including the original document of Queen Sophie Magdalene's foundation, gorgeously emblazoned, and a most curious specimen of the arts of the time. But there are, as well, at anyrate two full length portraits of Prioresses; one of them not so interesting because by an inferior hand, if formidable for width of crinoline and pastoral crook. The lady of the portrait is the first Prioress of Vallø, a German Princess who did not get on very well either with the ladies of the convent, or with the Royal Court, for five years only after the foundation she was back at Würtemburg-Neustadt where she came from.

But the other portrait is by Andreas Brünnicke again, and I am sorry indeed not to have seen it, for it is a full length version of that first seen head of a Prioress in the Frederiksborg collection. It is the same Princess of Sleswig-Holsten-Sønderborg-Glucksburg, and a collateral therefore of the present Royal Family of Denmark, and of the Duke of Edinburgh. In her portrait she points to the charter of the convent marked with Queen Sophie Magdalene's initials on the table before her, to the golden key, and to the Queen's

Princess Louise Sophie Frederikke of Sleswig-Holsten-Sønderborg-Glucksburg (1709–82). Prioress of Vallø

27 Vibeke Margrethe Juel (1734–93). Prioress of Vallø

Both from portraits by Andreas Brünnicke (1709–82)

28   Chalk cliffs at Rügen

From the painting by Caspar David Friedrich (1774–1840)

seal alike with her monogram upon it. If her crinoline be of the same rose-pink as the upper part of her dress in the picture of her at Frederiksborg, this must, indeed, be a delightful portrait, enhanced by the beauty of her ruffed sleeve, by the black lace, and by the way in which her jewelled Order and ribbon, white cravat, and sparkling earrings are rendered. In the twelve or thirteen such foundations for ladies of noble birth that exist in Denmark, and in the castles or manor houses that were those ladies' homes, there must surely be more of these portraits of Prioresses by Andreas Brünnicke, just as it may now be considered certain that portraits in Denmark that are exceptional for their clear colour of dress, and because of jewelled ornaments worn on the breast or shoulder, or in the hair, are by this forgotten painter. And thinking of these crinolined ladies with their fine croziers in their hands, a sort of northern echo to Pietro Longhi, and to more portrait painters as delightful in achievement and as unjustly forgotten as Raphael Mengs, the sun was already setting behind the woods of Vallø as we took the road again to Copenhagen.

After only a day spent away it is a pleasure to return there. More still after an absence of a few days when there has been time to miss the Tivoli Gardens and determine that during a month in Denmark one should be present every evening when the pantomime begins. For now we had begun to make excursions, not only to most parts of Zealand, but to Funen, too. Near, in fact, very near to the town, there are of course, more things to see, such as the Royal Hunting Lodge or Eremitagen by Lurids de Thurah in the park at Dyrehaven, small and modest with delightful statues lying on the gables and outlined against its mansard roof. Sorgenfri (Sanssouci in Danish) is a little palace or hunting pavilion which I did not see. Another journey, *in absentia*, was in order to visit Bothwell's mummy in the church at Faarevejle, far away in the left hand top corner of the island. It was disappointing not to get there, for we had approached as near as Jægerspris (see p. 41). Bothwell, who had been driven by storms from Orkney onto the coast of Norway, was brought prisoner by Rosenkrantz to Copenhagen; and I offer no excuse for taking the first opportunity to write down the Danish name, familiar to all Englishmen who are lovers of Shakespeare, only wishing there were time and opportunity to write of Bothwell's haunted marriage to Mary, Queen of Scots, of his brother the head of the witches who lived in exile in Italy, and his sinister friend and accomplice Dr. Fian, who plotted the death of James I and came to a witch's end. When wrecked on the Norwegian coast, Bothwell was already outlawed and under sentence of death from the Scottish Parliament for his part in the murder of Darnley. He had been imprisoned by the Danes for nine years when he was brought to the nearby castle of Dragsholm (now a hotel!), where he passed the last two years of his life. His mummy is said to be still recognizable as that of a handsome man in life, though Marryat looking for an account of Bothwell by a contemporary only found one by Brantôme, who saw him on his visit to Paris, describing him as "the ugliest and awkwardest of men", and agrees with Brantôme by declaring his corpse to be that of an "ugly Scotchman". A hundred years ago, when Marryat went to Faarevejle, the hair of the mummy was "red mixed with gray, that of a man about fifty years of age; the form of the head wide behind, denoting bad qualities; high cheek bones; remarkably prominent, long hooked nose, this may have been the effect of emaciation; wide mouth, hands and feet small, well shaped, those of a high bred man." And Marryat, after first severing a lock of Bothwell's red and silver hair as a souvenir, went on his way, *en route* as we ought to have been ourselves to Kalundborg to see the church built in the form of a Greek cross, a twelfth century brick building with no fewer than five octagonal towers each carrying a pointed spire. In silhouette this must be the most interesting building in all Denmark, particularly when seen from the water, which is easy enough as the ferry goes from there to Jutland, but it would seem the interest ends there and that there is nothing much inside. In photographs this church is reminiscent of the cathedral of Courtrai in Belgium with its *chonqs clotiers* as they are called in the Walloon dialect, which means its five square towers.

A prime object in coming to Denmark was to see its old

castles and manor houses which, proportionately, are as numerous as in England and are as important for the history of the country. A great number of them are in Zealand, the main island, though perhaps there are more still in Funen. A certain difficulty here presents itself to the writer because whereas it would only be possible to see all of these houses over many months or even years, there are instances in which he has received special permission and cannot therefore out of common courtesy write of them in such manner as to draw down crowds of English, and other tourists all clamouring for admission. I shall, therefore, say nothing of whether these houses are open or not to the public, and leave the reader to make his enquiries which if politely done, perhaps, seldom meet with a refusal. And this is the moment before setting forth on these expeditions to regret once more the destruction of what must have been the most splendid of all such houses in Denmark, Queen Sophie Magdalene's country palace of Hirschholm, once the Versailles of the Danes, pulled down and razed to the ground by Frederik VI, her grandson who, as well, sold all the contents having miserable recollections of his childhood there when attended by Struensee, his mother's lover who was a doctor by profession, and no doubt nightmare memories of his mother's imprisonment, of Struensee's execution and his own insane father, the mad King. But we can get at least an impression of Hirschholm from *Den Danske Vitruvius*. It had, of course, avenues and a splendid parterr'd garden, and many treasures in the way of furniture and pictures, but knowing the King's background it is not wholly possible to blame him. The date of Lurids de Thurah's *Den Danske Vitruvius* (1746–9) is a little early in the century and excludes many of the later houses, but it draws attention to Queen Sophie Magdalene and points to her as the greatest Danish builder of the century.

Bregentved, in about the middle of Zealand, is a fine large house rebuilt in eighteenth century style, with a good rococo chapel and splendid park of old trees, perhaps as fine as any in Denmark, the trees being now nearly two hundred years old and at their best. It is by a landscape architect as good as any in England in the time of Repton, and there are beautiful lakes and much use of water. In fact, like many demesnes in Ireland, it is to all intents and purposes an artificial landscape, hills and views altered, lakes dug, trees planted, as in a Chinese hunting park, all in the English influence which, it is true, had come from China by way of Sir William Chambers. The consensus of these 'English' parks all over Northern Europe is something not yet appreciated for its artifice, where all appears natural, but it is nature in leading strings and as artificial as anything ever accomplished by human hands. It is in this spirit that the park at Bregentved should be seen with its trees and glitter of waters, not the formality of the old French garden, but a work of art no less, to be admired and listened to upon an August evening when a cool air is in the leaves.

Another and more beautiful old house, Ledreborg, is not far away down an immense long avenue, built by Count Holstein who had been Prime Minister of Denmark early in the eighteenth century. This was the most Danish of the houses we had seen, typical of the country in its high dormer roof with two rows of attic windows in its plain wall surfaces, its obelisks with lamps, and plain pediment with coat-of-arms. That is to say, I would have known this house was not in Austria or Germany, and certainly it could not be in Holland. Formerly, as can be seen in old engravings, there was a French garden here of statues, terraces, and fountains, all swept away and landscaped in about 1830, the site of the old garden being the steep declivity below the house. There are some most curious pictures here; a Danish widow or two of the delayed Middle Ages unspeakably grim of demeanour, and a satire upon Luther, Calvin and the Reformers, with an Englishman, Perkins, who had been envoy from Queen Elizabeth, thrown in with them and given a place in the painting near the devil.

But the delight of Ledreborg is the large hall upon the first floor, somewhat recalling the Kaisersaal in baroque monasteries along the Danube and in Bavaria. Here for the first time we saw those Royal portraits which are so particular a feature of most Danish houses. At Ledreborg it is Christian VI, husband of Sophie Magdalene, with red heels to his shoes, and

29   Ledreborg, built by Count Holstein in the early eighteenth century

30   Frederiksborg Castle (1560–1620)

feet in the first position of dancing, right foot forward. The overdoors, as well, have graceful paintings. This was the prettiest room we had seen in Denmark, delightful in its pastel colours and firm and graceful in execution. There is a chapel of the same date, and long corridors with early portraits, many of them interesting for costume and for such details as the wearing of the thumb-ring. But this house has one exceptional treasure, a large miniature painting by Isaac Oliver which, seen in a Danish house, is all the more curiously English, although the painter was Huguenot in origin, his parents having fled with him from religious persecution in Rouen.* Is the river in the background a reminiscence of the Seine, one wonders! But it is clear that Oliver had studied Flemish paintings of the school of Brueghel, for there is the touch of that master in the gallows and telltale wheel upon the river bank. What are English are the ladies' dresses, not so much the staid group upon the left as the pair of revellers, one playing her lute, and her companion who pulls the sleeve of the reclining or drunken gentlemen, as though persuading him to dance with her. Their wanton necklaces and extreme *décolletage* being of the same order, none the less, as that in which the Virgin Queen gave audience to the Spanish Ambassador, and shocked him. But the gentleman plucks at her dress, listens to the music, and would have her stay with him. There is an exquisite and dewy tonality to this little painting which is a precious relic of the Golden Age. And one looked again at the lady lutenist and wondered if, perchance, she was singing one of Dowland's songs, who composed the second and third of his *Bookes of Songs or Ayres of foure Parts, with Tableture for the Lute* in Denmark, and inscribed his preface to the second book from Elsinore, 1 June 1600!

* He signed his miniatures Ollivier. This miniature at Ledreborg may be the finest of his paintings, other than his portraits, the best of which is probably the portrait of Richard Sackville, Earl of Dorset, in the Victoria and Albert Museum, in the style of Marcus Gheeraerts, his brother-in-law, but how English are his blue hose clocked with gold, galligaskins of rich embroidery, spare armour on the floor, the Turkey carpet, and 'Hardwick' matting on the floor! Walpole mentions several other subject pictures by Oliver, who died in 1617, but no clue as to the Ledreborg painting.

The time had now come to go and stay with our friends in Falster, or, in fact, at Gedser, which is the extreme southerly point of Denmark. We saw again the distant turrets of Vallø in the tall old trees, coming a little off the highway to call at Gaunø, the castle of the Thott family on its little island, filled from floor to ceiling with paintings. In the dining room there is that huge group of children with frizzed out flaxen hair, as fair as the Frisians; and there are other paintings beyond number including two or three by Frans Post, the Dutch seventeenth century artist who went to Brazil with Count Maurice of Nassan, builder of the Mauritshuis at The Hague, and painted pictures there. Returning to the highroad we were soon at Vordingborg and on the great bridge joining Zealand to the island of Falster, and to Lolland, too. This is an even more impressive work of engineering than the bridge from Funen to Jutland, and if there is too much water in Denmark it lies, at least, in fine, large stretches, not like the endless rivers and canals of Holland. It gives, to strangers at any rate, the feeling that on its far side they are entering a new land. There are, in fact, three southern islands, Falster in the middle, and Lolland and Møn to left and right hand; and we are now on the main road that leads, via the ferry over the Baltic, but some twenty miles, to Rostock, and to Germany. The point of land grows thinner, the road straighter and straighter among the pine woods, and at last we are at Botogården, near Gedser.

Nothing could be more charming than a welcome to a Danish house, and a family that includes a mother, her two sons and daughters, and her daughters' husbands and their children. It is, also, extraordinary how so many of them are staying in the house, and that there should be no bother about it all and room for everyone. Dinner, it is true, is a little early even by English standards—it is at seven o'clock—but there is so much to talk of that it goes by too quickly, and already on the way upstairs to bed one is regretting that there is only one more night to stay. Next day was Sunday, more and more relations and friends came to luncheon, and we had one of the most delicious meals that I have ever eaten beginning, of course, with a stupendous smørrebrød. It was a delightful wooden house, and I could not get it out of my head being a lover of nineteenth century Russia that we were staying in some Russian country house in the time of Turgeniev. I think, there, that the welcome would have been the same. And in the morning, seeing the small children picking cherries which were packed in barrels and sent straight off to Copenhagen to make cherry brandy, I wondered if one would not have seen the same thing in Russia, but the children were playing with the farmers' children, there was nothing feudal or subservient in anyone in sight, I thought of the Heering's Gard at Copenhagen where the hospitable proprietor gives bottles of cherry brandy to his visitors, and knew I was among the Danes. It was owing entirely to our friends at Gedser that we had come to Denmark, and perhaps we never felt ourselves so much in Denmark as with them.

In the morning and afternoon we drove into Lolland, which must be about the size of a small English county, seeing an old red brick *gåde* of the sixteenth century and many fine landscaped parks including that of Krenkeny. This is a flat and most fertile part of Denmark, and perhaps its riches are attested by the rebuilding of most of its old country houses during the last century with the restored Frederiksborg as model. There is the feeling in Lolland, as in Falster and in Møn, that you are on an island in the Baltic. Many of the place names in Møn and Falster, names such as Kramnitze, Tillitze, Corselitze, are not Danish at all but Wendish, and were brought in the Middle Ages by Wendish settlers from the heathen isle of Rügen, of which more anon. Lolland would seem to be one of those parts of the world where there is nothing much and everything. It is too rich and fertile for many of its old houses or villages to be left standing, and the present time is too busy to think back into the past.

While at Gedser, it was an amusing thought to be staying at one end of Denmark, its most southern point, and to think of The Skaw which is the fishing village between the Skagerrak and Kattegat at the extreme northern point of Denmark and the entrance to the Baltic. In a straight line the Skaw would seem to be some two hundred miles from Gedser, but in a guide book it gives the distance from The Skaw to Copenhagen as three hundred and one miles, making the journey, presumably, by road or rail, all the way round through Funen and through Jutland. Thinking of Denmark as being shaped like a triangle, it is about one hundred and twenty miles broad. But from Tønder to Copenhagen it is a little wider than that, and works out, once more, at a hundred and eighty miles. This gives us the dimensions of Denmark which, so much of it being water, is of about the area of Ireland.

And now for fair Liselund upon the island of Møn. We go over the great bridge again joining the islands to Zealand, and soon are lost in the woods and cornfields with an apprehension that we are arriving at a very special place, somewhere out of the ordinary world, or in a little world of its own. And let us imagine that we get out and leave the car for a few moments, and lie down upon a grass bank to rest, and think of what we have seen in Denmark, and fall half-asleep. But for its being an afternoon in August it could well have been one of those sandy shores of the Baltic, one has so often heard of, where lilies-of-the-valley are growing out of the sand at the water's edge. So much for the fair hair and blue eyes of the north, remembering the Mediterranean where asphodels grow in the plain of Paestum at foot of the classical temples, where there is the acanthus and the river-bed is full of red and white oleanders; or you can be rowed along the cliffs of Capri at five or six o'clock on a February morning, coming off the boat from Amalfi, and pick the narcissus from the cliff face as you go along. So the lily-of-the-valley is the flower of this shore and we think of picking them in handfulls, holding the bunches to our faces, becoming absorbed in them, thinking and seeing nothing else, breathing them in.

And all at once in the high wood behind us we hear the *tirra lirra* of a hunting horn, and another, and another, and then a pause while we sit up and listen, and suddenly a great beating of the waters, a flapping and a honking, and a line of swans comes round a headland out behind the trees. They are flying so low they only just clear the bank, and we hear the oaring, oaring of their wings as they gain height, and come back again flying straight over the lake, circling, once, twice, and then settling on the shadowed waters round an island. And now from both sides, and from below us, with a loud noise of rowlocks and a splashing and feathering of the sunset lake, boats and pinnaces appear each with a sportsman standing in the bow with a man to hold his powder flask and bag of shot. And the horns play again from the hanging wood behind the island, having moved position and come nearer.

After which, as though in a dream or hallucination, we see a pinnace painted in gold with a King standing in it, and a barge behind him filled with Court ladies. Time rolls back for a moment, and we see them picnicking two hundred and fifty years, or but an hour ago. The Queen and her ladies have come lumbering to the shoot in high-wheeled coaches, but two Princesses have come riding sidesaddle on long maned horses with a groom to lead them. They are just dismounting in their tricorne hats and long skirted riding habits. The martinet-like figure is the Arveprinds (Crown Prince) in his black armour, for he even goes hunting in half-armour, and we look closer at him in his great periwig, and know him with his long nose and jutting chin, and that we shall hear him knocking in the night upon the doors of Clausholm when he come to the sleeping palace to fetch away his 'conscience queen'.

The collation is laid out upon the grass, and there is a moment to admire the inlaid guns with silver locks that are taken from their masters as they sit down to eat. The ugly King in his periwig is served upon one knee by lacqueys in the red livery. And behind him the two Princesses talk to a fine young man who is the Gyldenløve, their half-brother. The Queen has a heyduck at her beck and call, in his fairy tale half flower-pot hat with its nodding flowers. But time moves forward. The sign for the massacre of the swans is given. All are on their feet again and climbing into the boats. They close in upon the island from both sides, and in a few moments have taken the swan citadel by storm. The white swans fall out of the sky, or are clubbed to death as they wobble awkwardly upon land. Not one is spared, goose, gander, or cygnet; but as the sun goes down in flames behind the trees, one swan beats along the water, and rises and flies over the hunting party, and into the sunset. And this swan princess has a golden collar on her long white neck, and the shape of her collar is a golden crown.

We have been watching a Royal hunting party. In the year 1692 King Christian V, with his Queen and many nobles, hunted the swans on their way from Møn to Nykjøbing, enjoying good sport, and slaughtering in one day four hundred and twenty wild swans near the village of Gjedsen. Molesworth, the old English writer, tells us of these swan battues, saying, "These wild swans haunt a small island about one mile distant from Copenhagen, and breed there. About this time of the year the young ones are near as big as the old, before the feathers are grown long enough for them to fly. The King, Queen, and the Court ladies, with other nobles, are invited to take part in this sport. Every person of condition has a pinnace allotted to him, and when they come near the hunt surround the place, and a great multitude of swans—sometimes a thousand—are killed. The flesh is worthless, but the feathers and down are preserved." So says Molesworth*; but we have placed our swan hunt not in Falster, but on the isle of Møn.

Here, the beechwoods are beautiful and we are approaching what is beyond argument the most interesting landscape in all Denmark. Møns Klint it is called, a tell-tale name in a land of which the other and northern extremity has names, Kattegat, Skagerrak, and The Skaw, that are so expressive of winter storms. Møns Klint means the Cliffs of Møn, but, first, you have to walk through Liselund, arriving through the beech trees at a vast half-timbered farm, the very epitome of a farm in Denmark, with huge interior piggery reminding one of the monk's dormitory in some great old monastery, except that though there is much snoring there is little or no sleeping, and that from another aspect nothing less like a monastery could be imagined, for the inmates are all enormous sows and their litters. The little piglets are running

---

* *Account of Denmark as it was in the year 1692*, by Robert, Viscount Molesworth. He was sent as Envoy extraordinary to the Danish Court in 1689 by William III.

round in circles on the straw, climbing over each other, darting away in fright if you so much as lift your hand, or lying drunkenly near to their mothers, milkbesotted, and once more, all said and done, it is like a monks' *dormitorium*, but a dormitory taken over for the pigs, and it must be added, administered for and on behalf of them as though it is the Ritz, or one of the Hilton group of new hotels. There is a huge old courtyard of farm buildings, and at the far side sundry signs such as pots of red geraniums in the windows betokening that it is possible to stay here. Delightful that must be, given the comfort and cleanliness of the Danes, and opening our travelling companion of a hundred years ago we find that Marryat stayed here only a few days later on 1 September 1860, when it was the harvest home.

"A cart drove into the court laden with sheaves of corn and peasants, male and female, shouting and singing. Horses, men, women, all were decorated with garlands of leaves and flowers, the latter bearing in their hands large bouquets stuck upon the ends of long sticks. Then, later, other carts decorated and begarlanded like the first, and a rustic Silenus, more horrid-looking than can be imagined, who approaching the farmer and his wife, according to ancient custom, sickle in hand, says:

"'We have cut the corn; it is ripe; it is gathered in. Will you now that we cut the cabbages in the garden?'

"'No, thank you,' reply the *hunsbond* and the *hustru*. 'We had rather not.'

"'But we will; the corn is gathered in; we will now cut the cabbages in the garden.'

"'No,' answers the master. 'As the corn is ripened and is gathered into the barn, we will give you a festival.'"

And there follows a bacchanale of innocent jollity.

But this is but the first part, or even the overture.

For coming through the court there is a beautiful walk down through the trees, down, down, till they open into green lawns and slopes, and little ponds and fountains, with rising ground all round hemmed in with trees; and looking down on this, but built low and under the hill, the thatched cottage of Liselund. It is an enchanting little building of 1790, a *cottage orné* with thatched roof, three dormer windows in the thatch, and below that a projecting portico with three windows, a window to either side. No less of an enchantment within; a fine, airy room in the middle looking down over the lawns, little rooms to both sides, and at the back a large and hidden dining room; staircase with lantern above it, and at least three love-nest bedrooms. Liselund must be among the prettiest of all *cottages ornés*, its only peer, perhaps, the Swiss Cottage in the green *demesne* at Cahir, in Co. Tipperary.

If you go down through the lawns, and climb up through the trees beyond, you find yourself approaching the third act or apotheosis of the fairy story, which is the sight of Møns Klint, or the Cliffs of Møn. But this is, and perhaps it is for the best, but the beginning of them, for they go on for several miles. They are chalk cliffs of fantastic formation, rising to more than four hundred feet high, which is equivalent to a range of Alps or Pyrenees in Denmark. They are like a line of chalky clouds or pinnacles. Scrambling to the top of one wood, and down another, and then up again, you reach a little level space or platform from which if you look to the right hand, there are visible the first of those chalky pinnacles or bastions. The Cliffs of Møn should, of course, be seen from a rowing-boat and looked up at from below as they lift their points and cones of dazzling whiteness against the blue sky. It is, indeed, a strange and haunting landscape, with only one thing in the world at all resembling it, which is the painting of *Chalk Cliffs at Rügen* by Caspar David Friedrich, and this is a little interesting to us because Caspar David Friedrich, though a German painter, studied at Copenhagen, and it is more than probable that he saw the Cliffs of Møn. This German Romantic of Romantics was born at Greifswald, an old town on the Baltic, just opposite the isle of Rügen, in 1774. He painted much in Rügen, an island with the same chalk cliffs as those of Møn; and indeed so near to it that from Arkona, the northernmost point of Rügen, Møn is clearly visible only some twenty miles away.

Of Rügen, unfortunately, there is not space to speak here, more than to note that before becoming a Russian launching ground for long distance missiles it had been a summer resort and, earlier, the legendary domain of the Princes of Putbus, lords of Schoritze, Dumsewitze, and Loebnitze—all Wendish names to be compared to the before mentioned Kramnitze, Tillitze, and Corselitze of Lolland and Falster—a family who claimed descent from Odoacer the Goth, of the nation by whom Rome was overthrown; and but to mention its ancient beechwood of Stubbenitze, and the Black Lake or Hertha See in midst of that mysterious grove, so called from the dark shadows of the surrounding beech trees. Tacitus describes this *castum nemus*, untrodden or virgin wood, where the chariot of the goddess Hertha was kept, drawn by cows and washed in a secret lake. At Rügen are great precipices of chalk of a character similar to those of Møn, the Stubbenkammer, in particular, more than four hundred feet high with steps cut in it, where "travellers", so an old book tells us, "repair to see the sun rise and set, and to enjoy the view".

It is these cliffs that Caspar David Friedrich painted, but on his way to and from Copenhagen it is almost certain that he went to Møn, for from Falster this is the quickest way to Stralsund and to his home at Greifswald. They are the Cliffs of Møn; as though painted by Caspar David Friedrich, and so I thought of them coming back through the green lawns of Liselund; passing a young man on horseback and hearing the owner was a Rosenkrantz of the romantic name, and another little thatched cottage which surely, must be that "small chalet", where, a hundred years ago, there was "a rustic kitchen, a long table and benches spread out before it, where a decent woman and her pretty dark-eyed daughter" kept a small restaurant. But the Danes, a nation of ballet lovers, will not mistake me if I call it the thatched cottage, to one side of the stage, where Berthe lives with her dark-eyed daughter, Giselle.

CHAPTER IV

Excursion to Skåne and a Note on Bornholm

IT IS, of course, enough to see the Swedish shore from Elsinore for it to become imperative to go there. One thing which is mysterious in classical history is the Roman failure to set foot in Ireland. For their legions had penetrated to places from which Ireland was in sight, there must have been sea-communication between Ireland and Wales and North Britain, and their intelligence service surely informed the Romans that Ireland was a small country and that nothing lay beyond it. The Romans were, for once, failing in curiosity. But having some memories of Southern Sweden from twenty years ago was a further inducement to go there, if any was needed, and we would have gone to Stockholm had not all the hotels been full. What an opportunity to see again the marvellous St. George and the Dragon in the Storkyrka by Bernt Notke, the China Slott at Drottningholm, the old theatre with its sets of scenery by Desprez, and Gustavus III's little pavilion at the Haga Slott, one of the most exquisite works of the whole eighteenth century, which, I think, was either closed to the public twenty years ago, or completely forgotten, or I would certainly have been there! But Stockholm was debarred. So it seemed best, instead, to try and see as much as possible of Skåne, particularly as this southernmost province of Sweden was part of the Kingdom of Denmark until 1659 and because, the region round Stockholm apart, Skåne has more castles and old houses than any part of Sweden. There was no question of going to Göteborg, for that city is much further north towards the frontier with

Sweden, it is not in the province of Skåne but in Halland, anyway, and because I knew Göteborg already and am no great admirer of the modern Swedish style.

We crossed, therefore, in the ferry from Copenhagen to Malmø in a wild downpour of rain and under leaden skies. It had not rained so hard on any evening in the Tivoli Gardens. Such a downpour was it that you got wetter from the rain splashing up off the pavement than from its soaking, sodden fall upon your back and shoulders. And having raised anchor, the rain was falling like a ringing or a jangling on the harbour waters, and so out into a mist of rain. All this in the middle of August; with two hours to try to find the difference between Danish and Swedish on a printed menu; and a filling of forms entitling one to buy so many cigarettes on the way to Sweden, and back, as though registering oneself as a drug fiend, together with slight but visible differences in the smørrebrød and smørgåsbord, as though adapted for another race of pelicans. Seeing, at last, the Swedish lightships and the buoys heaving and rolling in the summer sea, and arriving at Malmø where customs formalities—why are they called that? —were so informal that they were a matter of seconds, and we were made free of this enormous country, eight hundred miles long at the very least, and could if we wished, or had time, have gone right up to the Arctic Circle, and beyond, as far as Karesuando, in order to compare the Lapps of Sweden with the Lapps of Kautokeino, inland from the Alta-fjord in Norway, whom we had seen two years before. That must surely be a thousand miles from Malmø. But we drove, instead, to the hotel.

There is in Sweden, immediately, the sense that it is a huge country. Provinces, Blekinge, Värmland, Järntland, or Medelpad, of which one has hardly heard before, knowing only in any detail Dalarne, or Dalecarlia, where I had spent some time at Rättvik and Leksand, on Lake Siljan, in order to see the peasant costumes and observe the northern light, filtered as it were, through the birch woods, and something entirely novel and different from the Mediterranean light of Southern Italy and Spain. It is, also, apparent, as quickly, that Sweden is the most civilized country in the world, the fruits of having kept herself neutral for more than a century and during the two World Wars; advanced, that is to say, in matters of a perfect telephone system, clean electric trains, good bus-shelters, fine street lamps, and all for which Switzerland is famous, but better done. Switzerland is a polyglot land, speaking French, German, Italian, and the Ladin or Romontsch; it is unlikely that you will see any object except a watch or a cuckoo-clock and know from its style that it is Swiss, whereas the hand of Sweden is unmistakable, whether, or not, you admire the Town Hall at Stockholm, a Swedish chair or lampshade, or the Orrefors glass. There is a definite Swedish style, and that is apparent in every shop window, and in the lighting system in a hotel bedroom. It is obvious, also, in the objects in the shop windows, and perhaps nowhere more so than in the flower shops with their cult of indoor plants.

In so modern a town as Malmø it seems almost an anachronism to enquire about old castles and manor houses at the hotel desk. But they are the pride of Skåne and everyone knows their names, if not the quickest way of getting to them. The hotel porter, as if struck with a new craze, spent the whole morning and most of the first day on the telephone importuning the castle owners, and in the evening produced a 'bag' of names of old houses, as though weighing the day's catch and telling, meanwhile, his own fishermen's stories. In the end, we only dared to stop outside for a few moments, fearing the welcome, good or bad, within. The first stop was Lund upon a Sunday morning, Lund which was the *Londinum Gothorum*, of the same derivation as London, only about twenty minutes from Malmø with a Romanesque cathedral which, externally, has a beautiful arcaded apse, and in the interior, fine steps leading up to the transept and a splendid crypt or vault below. But everyone sat waiting for the clock to strike, which happened after a while and a little row of figures came out and moved by clockwork to an ancient tune.

After Lund we were deep in the landscape of Sweden, great sweeping plains of corn with clouds dragging their shadows after them and the country appearing to roll down in huge shelves and declivities towards the sea. Or was it only that we knew Sweden was so big a country? But it seemed to come down in vast curves and contours out of the distance, and it looked enormous compared to the straits and woods of Denmark! And presently not far from the cornfields we came a little off the road to Skarhult, our first castle in Skåne, built by Sten Starholt Robesparre, a Danish noble, rather resembling a castle in Scotland, but built of red brick with gabled ends to its roofs, and a formal garden of clipped hedges much in the style of Egeskov, but the house of a bigger landowner than Egeskov. Once and twice we stopped in front of it, not daring to stay longer, and then worked round to the west towards the shores of a biggish lake. One particularity of the province of Skåne is its large old inns, or sometimes they are only eating places and we had been directed to one of these for luncheon, finding it with difficulty, for it was not marked on any map and lay a considerable distance through fir woods off the main road. It proved to be a large wooden building with rooms decorated in peasant style, painted chairs, and much worked linen, and out of nowhere other parties appeared for luncheon and one could tell it must be well known for some miles round. But why in this remote situation? There was no village, and no other house in sight.

Early in the afternoon we were in front of another castle which I believe to be Vegeholm, but to tell the truth a great part of the pleasure of the few days we spent in Skåne lay in the delightful uncertainty of where we were. This is perhaps the more pleasurable to a normally, rather exact and precise mind, but, for once, I took no particular trouble to plan or remember anything, and we drifted from castle to castle through woods and cornfields. Vegeholm, if it was that, lies on an island in a moat, but its brick walls do not rise straight up out of the water, there is space on the island for walks and terraces. At the same time the island is dressed and cut round as though trimmed by the spade. Unlike Skarhult, which is three-sided with a formal garden in front of its open end, Vegeholm is four-square with an interior court. And now we turned south and came down towards the sea, but not to

the coast of Skåne which faces Denmark. We were making for
the south coast which is, in fact, opposite Rügen and Stralsund in Eastern Germany, reaching that coast at Ystad
where there are endless tramways or local lines which distract
attention and lead one time after time in the wrong direction
and away from the sea. After a long drive along the shore
eastward toward Falsterbo, a 'bathing resort' and 'artists'
colony', as though there were ever enough of any or all kinds
put together to make a colony! Mile after mile of sand and fir
tree, with no artist of any sort in sight, and depressing villas
and bungalows, for the Swedes go back to nature for their
holiday and mind not how uncomfortable they are. Then,
back down the long road through the fir woods, and so home
to Malmø.

Another day we started off in the same direction, coming
through Lund, and lost ourselves once more in the great
plains of corn. After a time there were trees, lime and beechwoods, and we were at the side of a large old country house,
not a castle, but a long, low, yellow building of late seventeenth
century date. This was Øvedskloster, and we walked to the
edge of the garden and looked back at it through arbours and
over clipped hedges and many apple trees. For once, it was a
fascination to know so little of the interiors of these houses,
or of the families who built them. And I remembered the
passage in Horace Marryat's two volumes on Sweden where
he retails the names of old Swedish families in a literal trans-
lation, names such as 'Lily Root', 'Lobster Helm', 'Lily
Hawk', 'Rosy Sunbeam', 'Rose Leaves', 'Bunch of Acorns',
'Northern Falcon', 'Reindeer Shield', 'Laurel Sunbeam',
'Laurel Mountain', 'Night and Day', with another family
who have for crest three black waterlilies. All affectations,
if we like to think of them as that, dating from the early
seventeenth century; but what, in fact, is a Reindeer Shield,
or a Laurel Sunbeam? How beautiful is the Danish name
Rosenkrantz, which means 'Crown of Roses', a rare thing
in Denmark where many of the old families have animal
names, Krag, Krabbe, Høg,* Gabel, Lange, and so on;
but the house of Oldenburg, on the other hand, had their

* But Høg means 'falcon'.

Gyldenløves, and in imitation of that the Royal bastards of the house of Wasa, who ruled in Sweden, were known as Gyllenhjelms, 'Golden Helmets'. Øvedskloster, on that sunny August evening, looked like the abode of Vertumnus and Pomona seen from the corner of the road where there was a limpid stream, and looking up through the espaliered trees.

Presently we came to another of the Skåne inns or eating places, a modern building of one storey with an immense dining room and a table of *smørgåsbord* in the middle of it, of a plentitude which would have caused a riot at half-term in an English boarding-school. There were eggs done in a dozen different ways, fresh fish and salt fish, sour cream and fresh cream, and it was an encouragement to watch about fifteen members of the same family at another table get up and help themselves again and again, while the waitresses bore down with reinforcements and put new dishes on the central table. The language difficulty was acute here. No one could even understand our few poor words of Danish. Swedish seemed an even more incomprehensible tongue than Polish. We had been told that August was the crayfish season in Skåne, beginning with a regular orgy or saturnalia of crayfish-eating on a particular day in August, but there was not a sight of a crayfish and on pronouncing the word *kraftør* again and again we were given to understand by signs that it was a bad season, that the crayfish, indeed, were behaving as the grouse on Scottish moors. The family at the next table, meanwhile, were ending their meal in unison with veritable salvoes or fusillades of pastry.

Next, we were in Helsingborg, an unattractive town, with all roads leading to Ramløsa whence comes the mineral water drunk all over Sweden. And on the way back along the coast from Helsingborg to Malmø we were delayed interminably by motor-races that gave opportunity to watch a Swedish crowd, and note their good looks, having been told so often that the Swedes and Italians were the beautiful races of the world. There was an extraordinary proportion of beautiful young girls, all well dressed and classless, affording no clue as to whether they came from the town or country. Many were riding pillion on motor-cycles; others standing by the roadside as crowds do in England, but their fair good looks seemed the rule, not the exception. We were stuck fast in an endless crocodile or caravan of cars moving at walking-pace and took an hour or more to cover the ten miles into Malmø.

There was one more day to spend among the woods and castles. A few of these are over at the far side of Skåne, where the coast faces east, and are some sixty or seventy miles from Malmø. Among them are Vittskovle, four-square on a trimmed and terraced island in a moat, and Trolle-Ljungby. But we took the direction of Helsingborg, and beyond, which is to say, parallel to Denmark and along The Sound as far as Kulla Gunnarstorp, where there are two castles, an old and a new, with Denmark plainly in sight when not blotted out by rain. Here, the shelving shore is too flat to be interesting, and there is too much road traffic coming from Göteborg. On this last day in Sweden one wished to go inland and be lost again. We made for the woods, which yet were nothing exceptional, being, hereabouts, like a Touraine without the vines, and after a long distance through that dappled shade reached what, comparing known and unknown with the help of photographs, must surely be the most beautiful of the old houses in Skåne. This is Vrams Gunnarstorp, which is in a different style from any of the others, in Dutch Renaissance, by all means, but, again, unlike any house that I have seen in Holland. Yet it is of the school of Christian IV's Stock Exchange in Copenhagen, and of Lieven de Key's red and white streaked Meat Market in Haarlem, neither of those being dwelling-houses, be it noted. The feature of Vrams Gunnarstorp are its gables on all sides, a little reminiscent, now we look at them, of the Riding School at Bolsover, but without the Cavalier spirit that informs those, and less aristocratic of appearance. The house would seem to have been very thoroughly restored, and perhaps some of its gabling rebuilt, or even added about a hundred years ago. The long line of window awnings gives to Vrams Gunnarstorp a flowering summer air, and it has water gardens and high, old, clipped hedges. Its interior court is said to be the finest part of the building, but this is not shown. We walked between hornbeam hedges and past stables and barns, all round the house, and left it with the feeling that it is a Dutch

110

town hall, or, at least, some urban building, migrant to Sweden, and put down among the woods and moats. A golden shaft of light touched one of the gables, recalling for a moment the brickwork of the Westerkerk at Amsterdam, the church by the Dutchman Hendrik de Keyser where Rembrandt worshipped and where his bones are buried.

But our most beautiful experience of Skåne was reserved for this late hour, for coming back towards Malmø we were in the marvellous northern woods. They are of another quality from the Danish beechwoods, and give the feeling that the roedeer could wander in them from here to Dalecarlia where the trees change to birch trees, and of a sudden we would see the first white peaked cap and the red and white dresses of Dalarne. These shadowy woods are full of mystery, and upon that evening, marvellous in their silence. And after mile upon mile of them, drinking in their cool and green draughts, there came a clearing and in the midst of that another castle. Here, to our great surprise and no little embarrassment, the house-owner, a young man, was waiting for us and without more ado took us upstairs to see oblong and oval rooms contrived out of the thick walls, graceful 'Gustavian' furniture in the French influence, and even harvest-festival paintings of the school of Archimboldo. His name we never discovered, and we only know that he is an ophthalmic specialist and married to the heiress of the castle. This was a treat we owed to the concierge, and our only opportunity to thank the owner; and next afternoon after a melancholy and rainy luncheon in another of the old Skåne inns at Vallinge, we came back by the ferry boat to Copenhagen.

One thing much to be regretted was that we could not get to the Danish isle of Bornholm, nearly two hundred miles away out in the Baltic. There the cottages, it appears, are red-painted, as in Sweden; there is much salmon fishing; and if one dare suggest it, too much pottery making. There are no old castles, but there are the round churches, whitewashed outside, and with pews and galleries within. Rønne is the capital of the island, and Østerlars is the best preserved of the round churches, with great buttresses and conical roof, looking a little like the curious, beehive *trulli* villages of

111

Apulia, near Bari. Of old there were other interests for which we have recourse to Horace Marryat, including Bornholm 'diamonds', worn like Bristol stone and Alençon crystals, for shoe buckles, or in the form of ornaments, as by Queen Louise, daughter of our George II, who appeared at a Court ball with a spray of Bornholm 'diamonds' in her hair, and was painted in them. Now, like Whitby jet, Bornholm 'diamonds' are forgotten. Marryat mentions, also, at a cattle show, the "very sturdy little bulls, small, like all island breeds", of Bornholm, and a day or two later attends a horse-fair, which is more interesting. "It must be", he says, "from these islands of the North that Franconi and the travelling circuses recruit their studs; for among the numerous *café au lait*, dun-coloured, flea-bitten, and other varieties, stood two geldings, as queer specimens of the equine race as ever mortals clapped eyes upon: black as the raven's wing, with four white legs—not stockings—white manes, with tails to correspond. It is said that somebody from the North presented four of these eccentric animals to Louis XIV, who was so pleased with their appearance that he had them harnessed to his own particular private gilded *caroche*." These horses would seem, unhappily, to have disappeared from Bornholm. But there are still reports of 'tigered' horses from Jutland or Apeloosas as they are called. Bornholm must have a rustic, Arcadian, piscatorial, and coloured character, all its own, and those who go there are enchanted with it. No less so than with the Swedish island of Gotland, with its ruined Gothic churches, its town walls of Visby and its climbing roses. One could be tempted further into the Baltic to look for the dwarf horses of Öland, another Swedish island, smaller than Shetland ponies, so small that they could be lifted with one arm. Gustavus III gave a team of Öland ponies to Catherine the Great, who drove in the gardens at Tsarskoe-Selo with them. And further still to see the ships and frescoed churches of the Åland islands, half-way between Sweden and Finland. It was bad enough to have missed Bornholm, an island which the Danes hold in particular affection, of which all reports are pleasant and one never hears complaint.

CHAPTER V

Funen, its Landscapes and Old Castles

B<small>ACK</small> to Funen, which is sad enough in itself, because Funen is on the way home. But this chapter is the result of three or four journeys thither: on arrival in Denmark, a couple of trips from Copenhagen, and another stay there at the end, by which time the classless ferry from Korsør to Nyborg had become more familiar than the cross-Channel steamer. During the course of these several visits we must have been nearly round the island; and if Falster is about the size of a small English county, then Funen is as big as two of them put together, say, Derby and Nottingham laid side by side, for it is some fifty or sixty miles both ways across.

It was on Funen, before reaching Copenhagen, that we saw our first Danish country house. But, for the sake of continuity, all impressions of Funen are resumed together into this one chapter, excepting Odense, which has been written of elsewhere. This first of the old manors was Glorup. Driving the long way round it in order to see something of the island we had stopped in a beechwood by the blue waters of the Little Belt and watched a great flight of wild duck overhead. And when we got to Glorup it was to find a numerous company of country gentlemen from all over the island, and even from Taasinge and Langeland, other isles, assembled to go shooting. We must have sat down at least twenty in number to our first experience of smørrebrød in a private house. Glorup is a large, square built mansion of 1690, with interior courtyard, long lime avenues, and a great formal canal or fish pond. In the interior are interesting Napoleonic relics, owing to some family link or connection with the Bonapartes, and presentation portraits of Napoleon III and the Empress Eugénie. Here, too, was the first portrait by Pilo that we saw in Denmark. And by the time we had seen the house the sportsmen had taken their guns and gone off shooting. It was a little like Edwardian shooting parties that I remembered in my childhood, but made more romantic by wondering what country houses and swan-haunted lakes they had come from, and would go back to on that August evening.

The same afternoon we went to Egeskov, one of the oldest and most beautiful of the Danish castles, and in a style peculiar to Denmark, for it is not quite the same thing that you see in Southern Sweden. Egeskov comes straight up out of the waters of the lake, not built on an isle or islets, as is Frederiksborg, but built, it is said, on oak piles or stakes driven home in the lake bed. There is, it is true, something of North German Baltic style in its stepped gables, some touch of Lübeck or of Stralsund, but, there, it would be in churches, not in houses. Typical North German houses are not in this manner. Nothing of the kind is to be seen in Lübeck, or in Bremen. Egeskov was built in about 1550, it would be much earlier than that were it an English building; and looking at it again we see it has but little of the original fenestration. The windows are long, like windows of the William and Mary period in England, and it is a safe guess, therefore, that the interior of Egeskov has work of that date, and this is borne out by its formal garden. It is true that one of the delightful features of the Danish houses of this period, and of their equivalents in Skåne, is the ease and skill with which work of this later and more comfortable date was installed into these earlier buildings. In the result their interiors have the harmony of two or three centuries flowing into one another, and such houses are most habitable in spite of domestic troubles which make it difficult, if not impossible, to have the evening meal later than half-past six or seven o'clock, and in Sweden earlier still, for the usual hour is six. In fact, Danes have finished their dinners before Spaniards have begun their teas. Were one asked in what the Danish houses differ from country

32　Vrams Gunnarstorp Slot, Skåne, built in 1632

33　Fredensborg Royal Palace

34 (*above*) The Ryber Family (1789)

35 (*left*) Mrs Bruun Neergaard with her elder son (*c.* 1790)

Both from paintings by Jens Juel

houses in England, or elsewhere, it would be, first and fore-most, in the family portraits. The earliest of these, which date from the sixteenth century, have a robust strength and ugliness, whether of bearded knight or widow, which removes them from the pomander-holding gallants of Queen Elizabeth, with their earrings, their scented beards, and tapering hands. The "old loyal custom" of hanging portraits of Kings and Queens of the house of Oldenburg in the principal room gives dignity and a fairy tale improbability because of the peculiar dynastic physiognomy of the family, which is exactly that a great illustrator or stage designer would invent. That the Northern Kings were even more popular because of their inherited features, and that it became a source of pride to their subjects, is not only the kind of patriotism that is easily understandable but is established fact. Family portraits of the Karel van Mander, Abraham Wuchters school, seem to show the emigrant Dutchmen confronted by personalities, male and female, even bigger than themselves, in rare instances with that frizzed fair hair. And the typical interior of an old Danish country house can be made complete with a huge old Danzig cabinet or two, some graceful furniture under French influence from afar, and later portraits that if they show a predilection on the part of the painter for jewelled ornaments on the breast and in the hair are probably by the forgotten Andreas Brünnicke, or if they are in Biedermeier style and later still will be by Jens Juel.*

Egeskov looks as though it has a history, rising out of its lake, and in the church of Kvaerndrup may be seen the *epitaphium* of Laurids Brockenhuus, lord of Egeskov, who according to legend, but on this occasion truthful, bricked up his unmarried daughter because she had given birth to a son, who was taken from her; bricked her up in a room with only a little opening left for food to be passed in where she stayed for five years till her father died and her brothers let her free. The *epitaphiums*, both to this gentleman and his father

---

* Jens Juel, born in Funen in 1745, studied in Rome and worked for some years in Paris. He died in 1802. He painted innumerable portraits and portrait groups, and can be seen in the national museums and in most Danish houses, e.g. Glorup.

Frands Brockenhuus, are as crowded with heraldry as any of the tombs in the glorious chapel of the Rosenkrantzs at Rosenholm, but their effigies are excessively curious. Frands, the father of the immurer, is in full armour with battle-axe on his shoulder, and great moustachios; by his side his wife stands with folded hands, for they are represented as standing, not lying down. Laurids, fat and enormously florid in his effigy,* has, too, his housekeeper-wife beside him, resigned to her fate and already in widow's weeds, as though he had predeceased her. The interior of Egeskov is not shown, and looking over the lake to it we may imagine for ourselves its old and fading portraits receding every year further away from us back into time. But there is at Egeskov one of the most beautiful of the old Danish gardens—on the mainland for there is no space for tree or flower—complete with lime avenues, maze, and clipped hornbeam hedges, laid out in about 1730. Here one may walk, looking out at the drawbridge leading into the castle, and contrasting the two ages, that of the battle-axe and the long peruke or periwig falling to the shoulders. They were making hay in every direction the day we went to Egeskov, down to the water's edge, and that age-old process of stacks and farm carts and hay forks filled in this picture of the flight of time.

On another day we went deeper into Funen in order to see another castle, that of Hesselager. This, too, has a moat round it, is of red brick, and of what in England we would call the Tudor age; though no house of pleasure, as those were then beginning to be built in England, for Hesselager is still for defence, and as though in constant expectation of attack. Hesselager is of redder, more mulberry-coloured brick than Egeskov, and has black and white, magpie farm buildings of the utmost picturesque interest to one side. This is something

---

* Some weeks after penning this description of his appearance I discover that Laurids Brockenhuus was "violent and ungovernable, and so strong that, when he rode out of the gate of Egeskov, by clasping a beam he could lift both himself and his horse from the ground, and blow a horn that hung there." Perhaps the picture is complete when we read that he married a daughter of Peder Skram, "Denmark's Daredevil".

entirely of Denmark; and it is remarkable how in even so simple a vernacular as half-timber buildings the eye can differentiate, immediately, between those of Normandy, or Denmark, or the black and white of Worcestershire, or of Warwick. You never see such immense ranges of black and white farm buildings as in Denmark; always with thatched roofs, and that these are a national feature is amusingly apparent in Lurids de Thurah's *Den Danske Vitruvius*, so often and gratefully mentioned in these pages, wherein these thatched magpie buildings, relics of the earlier tradition, appear side by side with the later and more graceful products of the rococo.

This particular excursion we completed by a long drive which took us practically all round Funen. We came back again through the beechwoods where the day before we had watched the wild duck flying overhead. This land of lakes and woods requires a legend and a background, and perhaps the writer is not the only person seeing it who has had the music of *Le Lac des Cygnes* continually ringing in his head. The stage direction reads '*l'Allemagne dans le temps des Comtes*', and if we advance this, imperceptibly, into Sleswig, and then Sønderborg, and then Augustenborg, we have arrived and are, indeed, in sight of Funen. Denmark is, surely, the land of *Le Lac des Cygnes*. And now, thinking of that, we come through the beechwoods to another and larger old castle of rather different character, which is Brahetrolleborg. Here, we penetrated into the church and far enough to see the castle courtyard. All round is a beautiful landscaped park of about 1830. Brahetrolleborg is a pleasure house and not a fortress, and it was sad not to be able to see the interior, where Marryat mentions "grand and spacious rooms" and portraits of the sovereigns of the house of Oldenburg. So we continued on our way by swan-haunted lakes and waters back to Odense.

Upon another occasion we came straight from Copenhagen, missing the ferry at Korsør and finding at the last moment that another and reserve one had been pressed into service, a veteran which many of the passengers greeted with pleasure because they remembered it when they were children. Our way led across Funen, through Odense and down through orchards of red apples towards great woods at the far side of the island, lying along the waters of the Little Belt, with the mainland of Jutland in sight. It was a little like looking from Anglesey into Caernarvonshire near Bangor, where the woods of Plas Newydd and Vaynol face each other across the Menai Strait. We were on our way to Wedellsborg, through more woods, and, presently, under an arched gateway and down an avenue till the long white house comes into view. Built like a long letter L, but the other way round so that it is shaped like a ⌐̄, with two immensely long white wings, and no particular central body, but all white wings. Within, a grand air of magnificence, and three or four *chambres de parade* leading into one another, splendidly furnished, and showing the acme of taste on the part of the owner, with inventions of his own devising such as a marble obelisk, two or three feet high, hung with eighteenth century miniatures, giving a superlative effect of luxury and grandeur. This enfilade of rooms with its fine portraits achieves the air of a palace out of a long plain white building. Elsewhere are bedrooms the decoration of which is achieved, quite simply, with vertical and horizontal strips of floral, or patterned Victorian wallpapers, as if panelled. There are, as well, portraits of Kirsten Munk, morganatic wife of Christian IV and three of her daughters, all in scarlet red and farthingales and gold-powdered hair; and a painting of Christian IV, in the chapel, lying on his death-bed, trussed up and swathed in scarlet and tied up in bows, as though, which was the truth, ready to be despatched on a journey without end. There is, also, one of the Danish bronze horns, or *lurs*, found near here, which should, on Midsummer Night, play of itself and sound a warning note. We slept in two rooms with private salon between, hung with a pair of Royal portraits, *le front fuyant* much in evidence, from the hand of Pilo. Wedellsborg has, decidedly, an air of magnificence which is, really and truly, the effect of cleverness and good taste of a high order, and while of Denmark in every particular it cannot fail to remind a visitor of staying at Łancut in Poland as the guest of Count Potocki. That this has been accomplished by relatively simple means is the measure of the owner's talent in arrangement which must have in it some proportion of stage sense. Perhaps this is the most sympathetic interior of any house in Denmark.

The reader must try not to tire of castles and country houses, for there is not much else in Funen. It was, then, from Wedellsborg that we started out on an afternoon on our way back to Copenhagen, and went down to the far south of the island, as far as Svendborg, a little town with a long curving street and large old posting-inn. But although it is built on the sea, the waterfront is elusive and not easy to find, till eventually you come down to it over several railway sidings to find the island of Taasinge immediately in front of you and but a few hundred yards away. But Taasinge is not the only island. There is the bigger isle of Æro, an hour and a half away by ferry, with the town of Ærøskøbing, said to have many old houses and to be the resort of retired sea-captains—one of the village churches has a painted reredos with the Apostles modelled on Marstal skippers, Marstal being the name of the village—and in Ærøskøbing, itself, is there not the museum of model ships, with five hundred ships, no two alike, in glass bottles? In short, the isle of Æro may well be, as it boasts, an isle of enchantment, and there is, surely, good polyglot entertainment there of an evening in conversation with old mariners.

But we are bound for Taasinge, a transit of ten minutes, no more than that, and we are among its apple orchards. It gives the impression in August of an apple island, and must be more lovely still in apple blossom time. It is the matter of a few moments, in this small and delightful island which is only some six miles across, before the road comes in front of Valdemar Slot. This is of advantage to passers-by, if detrimental to those to whom the house belongs, and it is a pity the road could not have been contrived, somehow, upon the other side. But it is never likely to be altered now, and it does at least impart to everyone, Dane and foreigner alike, a worthy impression of one of the most beautiful of the old Danish castles. Horace Marryat cannot agree to this, and describes it as "an ugly pile of brickwork", but then I remember, myself, when young, being told by an elderly female relation that Blenheim was "a vulgar pile". Not that Valdemar Slot at all resembles Blenheim but, at least, it is a building that is not trying to conceal itself but appears to be proud of its history. It is, I would rather say, distinguished and noble in bearing as we pass in front of it along the road which so rudely cuts it off from its formal canal and from the fishing-pavilion or summer house facing it at the far side. By kindness of the owner, for it is not generally open to the public, we were allowed inside. Valdemar Slot was built by Christian IV in about 1640 and given by him together with the apple isle of Taasinge as appanage to his eldest son by Kirsten Munk, Prince Valdemar, an unruly character who after a lifetime of trouble and intrigue died fighting in Poland, having become an officer in the Swedish army. Later, it became the property of the Juel family, descendants of the famous Admiral Niels Juel, to whom it still belongs. There are many and admirable paintings here, and a marvellous air of ancient grandeur that transmutes to poetry, and in the result is the history of a country.

As we would expect, there is a room of portraits of the house of Oldenburg; and Marryat is worth quoting, who remarks that "all are on horseback; each horse, however, follows that of his predecessor, giving the whole the appearance of a Royal carousal, or merry-go-round". And he calls attention to Frederik III (1648–70), son of Christian IV, who, as "*cadet du sang*, began life as Archbishop of Bremen, but painted *à cheval*, armed cap-à-pie, distinguished alone from his brothers by the starched ruff of the Lutheran clergy"; and to portraits of Niels Juel, the Admiral, "first as a boy, in red jacket and silver buttons, something like that worn at a Spanish bull-fight, and later surrounded by his victories, as Admiral, Knight of the Elephant, etc., a table with the names of his vessels, his captains, lieutenants, and officers down to the lowest grade". And Marryat concludes: "But of all the portraits of the Juel house, there is one most charming, a lady of the last century, missal in hand, coming out of church, the light of a setting sun falling on her dress through the mullions of a Gothic window, one of those effects of light so much loved by some of the Dutch painters; the master unknown." But this is a matter to which we return later.

For, in the meantime, in the corner of one of the smaller rooms was exactly what we had hoped to find since coming to Denmark, a portrait of a young Abbess: to be precise, Vibeke Margrethe Juel (1734–93), Prioress of Vallø, painted in 1752 when she was, therefore, eighteen years old, Andreas Brünnicke being the artist. She has the true flaxen hair of the Dane, so fair that it almost resembles a powdered wig; false ringlets falling from her shoulders; an ornament of pearls and diamonds worn jauntily a little to one side of her front hair; pearl earrings that must be convent property, for we notice what are surely the same pearl earrings in Brünnicke's portrait of a Prioress that still hangs at Vallø; a ravishing bow of lace at her neck and under her chin with ends cascading down her chest; ribbon and cross of the Order; and gorgeous lace cuffs tied with ribbons of black lace. But no crozier or pastoral crook, as though she has, at least for the moment, laid that aside for other duties; and a coat or, rather, tunic of almost military cut, suggesting that Cherubino has been gazetted cornet in some fantastically elegant corps or bodyguard. It is, indeed, a most ravishing portrait of a young girl. How beautiful to see her moving, coming into the room, dressed like that! She wears the veil of a Prioress, and must have been wearing a full hooped skirt. We hear the rustling of her dress as she turns round; and see her once more loaded with lace and jewels, and eighteen years old—it is a fascination, in itself, to see so many jewels worn by a young girl—ornaments, hoped for, but seldom seen, like the button-hole and fancy waistcoats worn at Eton on the Fourth of June, for this Prioress does personify what one individual at least, as a schoolboy, would have wanted his friend's sisters to look like. We leave her reluctantly, looking back over our shoulder at her, relieved to think that Casanova never met her!*

On a higher floor, at the top of a staircase, are the splendid

---

* She was not a Prioress for long. When twenty-four years old she married Caspar Christopher Brockenhuus, and in 1770 Hans Ahlefeldt, dying in 1793.

pair of Royal portraits of two Queens of Denmark, both by Pilo. They are immediately impressive because of their hooped skirts, being two of the best crinoline portraits known, and because of the splendour of their gilt frames. One of the Queens is beautiful, the other not; and the beautiful one is Queen Louisa, daughter of our George II, married to Frederik V. The year she died, he married Queen Juliane Marie, a princess of Brunswick-Wolfenbüttel, who is the second portrait. Queen Louisa, it must be said, has the best looks of any of the Hanoverians until George IV in his days as Florizel. She holds her head well, and is of noble bearing. The billowing crinolines in both portraits are of great effect, and the mean features and ugliness of the second Queen are almost redeemed by this.

It is time, now, to say a word on the subject of Carl Gustav Pilo, a painter almost unknown outside Denmark and Sweden. He was born in Sweden in 1711, but lived in Denmark for some thirty years from 1741. He could be a routine portrait painter, but, also, he could paint exceptionally, and we had already seen one of his best portraits in a private house in Copenhagen,* a dark green portrait—green seems to have been Pilo's favourite colour—a painting as good as an exceptional Allan Ramsay, for that is about his level. At Valdemar Slot there hangs, as well as the pair of Royal portraits, what is known as *The Moonlight Portrait*, of Anna Margrethe Juel, perhaps a younger sister or a niece of the Prioress, painted in about 1760, and this, I think, must be the picture Marryat refers to of a lady, "missal in hand, coming out of church, the light of a setting sun falling on her head through the mullions of a Gothic window, one of those effects of light so much loved by some of the Dutch painters", etc. But the memory of Marryat is at fault. The lady holds a fan in one hand and a workbag in the other, and it is the moonlight that falls on her through a square-paned window. It appears she died young at only twenty years old, and there is a little ghostly air about her picture. Other of his paintings do not rise above mediocrity. The portrait that we saw in Copen-

* Portrait of Mogens Skeel van Plessen painted 1744–9 (Mrs. Louise Hasselbalch, Copenhagen).

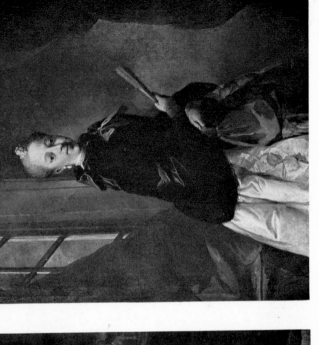

36   Anne of Denmark (1574–1619)
From the portrait by Paul van Somer
Reproduced by Gracious Permission of
H.M. The Queen

37   Anna Margrethe Juel (1741–61): the "moonlight portrait", in Valdemar Slot, by Pilo

38 The Coronation of Gustavus III of Sweden in the Storkyrka, Stockholm

hagen, as we said, is as good as an Allan Ramsay, and is in the French manner practised by that painter, for which reason it resembles, also, pictures by the Swedish artist, Roslin. But, in his pair of Royal portraits at Valdemar Slot, Pilo shows of what he is capable, and achieves something a little transcendental and out of the ordinary in *The Moonlight Portrait*. He seems to have seen earlier portraits of the Oldenburg family in the way we look at them, ourselves, and to have set out to exaggerate their small physique and extraordinary physiognomy. In one pair of portraits of Frederik V, and one or other of his queens, Pilo is known to have painted them, as it were, in green caverns or grottos of ice achieved by a green light on the curtains and draperies in order to give a northern effect, and perhaps give accent to Norway, Iceland, and Greenland being the dominion of the Northern Kings. But in 1771 Pilo quarrelled with the Academy at Copenhagen and returned to Stockholm in time to paint the huge, unfinished canvas of *The Coronation of Gustavus III*, his biggest and most ambitious composition. Large in planning, and with its multitude of portraits, this is the most important picture of the Scandinavian school—though the fact that Pilo left it unfinished shows, surely, that he was not satisfied with it—and a most interesting relic of the playwright-King who was so dramatically murdered as he left the Opera House. Of how many portraits there may be by Pilo in private collections in Sweden I have no knowledge, nor of their quality, for he lived there for another twenty years, dying in 1793. But there must certainly be more good portraits by him in Denmark, and in all three northern countries Pilo can be, on occasion, the painter worth looking for. Here, in Valdemar Slot, perhaps we see him at his best. He is certainly an abiding memory from that old house.

It would have been pleasant to continue into Langeland, which, indeed, is a long island, for it is some forty miles from end to end, and only twenty minutes or half an hour by ferry from the island of Taasinge where we are now. It is flatter than Taasinge, well wooded, with many orchards, too, and manor houses in plenty towards its northern end, including Tranekaer. One of the delights of Denmark, in spite of the complaints of its inhabitants, must be this possibility of 'island hopping'. From Rudkøbing, the capital of Langeland, if you but cross the island, which is scarcely more then five miles, you can take another ferry to Nakskov in Lolland in an hour and a half. In this way, for instance, a friend with whom we stayed in Jutland was able to start off in his car, come down through Funen to Langeland and to Lolland in order to attend a wedding, and return a couple of days later by way, first of Copenhagen, then Funen, and then back again. And, of course, if going to Jutland from Copenhagen, say to Aalborg, no one thinks of going by road, they all take the night boat and are there next morning. In this way there is much internal circulation in Denmark, a greater circuit, and as it were, some inner ones. It is this which gives internal life to the country, and helps the understanding of why Denmark is the second oldest kingdom in all Europe. Before the invention of steam, distances were enormously enhanced by the difficulty of going by sail, of having to wait days or even weeks because of contrary winds, and so forth; and the country was in effect, therefore, larger than its own size, though an immensity of lakes and isles and straits which was no more than the length of a little finger on a map of the whole world. We could have gone back this way to Copenhagen, through Langeland, Lolland, Falster, all of which could be traversed easily on a long day, but there was not time. We had to return to Copenhagen as quickly as possible, do a few things we had left till last, and start off for home.

We were to stay the night before going to Jutland at Gyldensten, an old castle near Bogense on the northern shore of Funen. It was a sad experience to come down for the last time to Korsør, eat an excellent luncheon on board the ferry, and get to Nyborg only in order to have our autographs collected by the same children for about the tenth time. Once more through Odense, now as familiar as our English county town, trying, in order to while away the time, to compare Denmark with its isles to Greece and the Greek Islands, with Langeland for Euboea, Funen and Zealand for Crete and Cyprus, and the whole of Jutland for Greece, proper, and the Peloponnese. Lolland, Falster, and Møn for the Cyclades and Sporades; or the Ionian Islands? And now we were in view of the sea again, looking towards the island of Samsø, but that was twenty miles away and out of sight; and had come down to Bogense and were but a mile or two from Gyldensten.

This is through a little wood, in midst of which you perceive the castle roof, and down a clearing into an immense three-sided court of magpie stables and farm buildings with gabled doorways and high, thatched roof of reeds. On the far side of the quadrangle stands the old brick castle in its moat; a sixteenth century castle and the barns, though it may be more than once rebuilt, are of the same date. But they are in peasant speech with a thick accent, whereas the castle talks to you in another tongue, of owners who have been to court, have heard Italian music, and seen ambassadors from Queen Elizabeth and from the King of Spain. Their house or castle, though in traditional Danish style, is like a Renaissance chest or cabinet bound in, as though by clasps of brick, and so tall and compact that it could be strapped onto a giant horse and taken away. All of one piece as to the exterior, that is to say, as if the work of a single lifetime, with hooded roof like the lid of an old trunk, tall and of many storeys, as if to look out through the trees, catch the sea air, and perhaps keep an eye along the sandy shore.

Within the castle the eighteenth century has left its mark of elegance, making it into a most habitable dwelling with rooms looking out on the further side onto a widened moat, the size of a small lake, beyond which are the gardens. And all round, it is enclosed by tall old trees. Again, as in other old castles, there are two or three rooms of this date opening into one another, giving, as thick castle walls do, the pleasant sensation of being as warm in winter as it is cool in summer. Rooms of an elegant and courtly air with many portraits of men in periwigs and tie-wigs, and ladies, young and old, with powdered hair. Also, numerous miniatures shown off against velvet backgrounds, and an equestrian portrait of Frederik V by Pilo for good measure. Here, we were able to talk of mutual friends, and to discuss the latest books more openly than in many English country houses, for our hosts had read the books and were not relying on opinions in our 'national' newspapers. Conversation ranged from happy times as an Oxford undergraduate to memories of London as it was before the First World War, and we looked at all the objects and the fine furniture, relics of an age and of a civilization that in England as in Denmark, to no one's benefit, is slowly dying out. Our hostess, whose sister we had stayed with only a few days before, like all Danes of our generation, had affectionate memories of London and of England. But perhaps the most delightful half-hour of the whole evening was when, at about ten o'clock and some hours after dinner was over, a tray was carried in and put down on a table, and we sat down to a typical Danish supper of raspberries and red currants, eaten with brown sugar and whey, the favourite dish, *rødgrød*, exactly, of Queen Alexandra, whom our hostess and her two sisters so well remembered; and one understood that this dish was a typical thing of Denmark in its simplicity, and wondered how often through the ages the castle inhabitants had sat down of an evening, after talking, and eaten *rødgrød*. Then, a little more conversation and it was time to go to bed. Falling asleep, one had pleasant and warm visions of the old and unhaunted castle of Gyldensten in its lilied moat.

CHAPTER VI

Jutland

WHEN we left Gyldensten we were on our way to
Jutland, over the long bridge back onto the mainland
of Europe. Danes will tell you that Jutland, or
Jylland as they call it, is the heart of Denmark. And in so
small a kingdom this should be true of a land mass or
peninsula two hundred miles long and, at its widest, a hundred miles across. Jutlanders pride themselves on coming
from Jutland, and there is the same local patriotism that
makes natives of Yorkshire, or East Anglia, or the West
Country, think, and say, that their's is the best part of
England. The porter in the hotel will become interested on
hearing you are going to Jutland and tell you there is no
place in the world like Aarhus. This, if he comes from a village
in the sand dunes many miles from the town.

Most of the Danes know enough of history to be aware
that the Jutes over the centuries made piratical descents
upon Great Britain. All of them have heard of King Canute.
Thus, Jutland is remote, but at the same time not out of the
world. Was not the Varangian bodyguard of the Byzantine
Emperors recruited from Jutland, out of Thyland or Thule, at
the remotest end of the land? So it has been said. The county
of Thy being over the Limfjord, and as far away as you can
go over the dunes. To have been in Denmark without going
to Jutland is equivalent to being in Spain without going to
Castile. And not to have seen the sand dunes is to have left
France before seeing a vineyard. Jutland, more than the
islands, is the true character of Denmark, its mainland and
body or heart, if not its mind. For Jutland is, of course, the

131

land of the jarls or peasant farmers. But, in fact, the dunes are only at the extremity of Jutland and there are woods and cornfields, but not as many lakes upon the way.

There is perhaps something particularly intriguing in arriving in a new country along a bridge, or through a tunnel. Think of the first moment of coming out of the Simplon into the Italian sunlight! And of course the supreme example is the causeway into Venice. It is the land connection that makes the difference. By the same principle, you are more aware of height looking down from a tall building than in an aeroplane. That is because you follow down the line of building with your eye, and there is direct physical contact between you and the earth below. Going by air or water you are in another element, But a bridge or a tunnel takes you there by earth; and yet because a bridge leads over the water and a tunnel digs underground it is a more impressive arrival than merely getting to the frontier. By coming over a bridge you are making use of two elements at once. And now, conveniently forgetting all mention of either the Simplon Tunnel or the causeway into Venice, for going to Italy and arriving in Venice is not, fairly, to be compared to coming to Jutland, let us say that there is one comparable sensation, which is the causeway over the Zuyder Zee from North Holland into Friesland. For Friesland has an individuality of its own and is not the same as Holland. Neither is Jutland of the same character as Zealand and the Danish islands. It is the mainland of Denmark, and not having been to Jutland you do not know the Danes.

By now we are in the middle of the bridge, which it is impossible not to contrast in one's mind with Telford's suspension bridge over the Menai Strait. And in another moment we are in Jutland, the lower neck of which at about its narrowest point we have crossed before, coming from Ribe to Kolding on our way to Copenhagen. But, now, we turn north and Fredericia is the next town, of old a fortress, because it secured communication between Jutland and the Danish Islands and was one of the strongpoints of the whole kingdom. In the Middle Ages, and later, Elsinore and Fredericia were the keys of Denmark. And Fredericia has still its ramparts, but little else of any interest save for those who have their homes there. And we go on half an hour to Vejle, more beautiful in situation, on a fjord, coming down to it through some lovely woods and finding a church which has been heavily restored. Not much at Vejle, though the guide book gives the Ritz and the Moulin Rouge for cabarets, and under the mention of hotels puts, appetizingly, Chateau-briand steaks and "the black Pot". But one of the mysteries of the smaller Danish towns is their night life. Even a little town in the south of Funen had its Don Juan-Casanova night club. In Denmark, proportionately to its size, there must be an enormous population of itinerant night club entertainers and cabaret 'artists'. Along the main street of every town you see their photographs in shop windows. What on earth can they do in winter, for most of these are summer places? No country that I have ever been to, except Roumania, has so many night clubs. French provincial towns are as sabba-tarian Scotland in comparison. It is true, if this has anything to do with it, that in Copenhagen there is the best permanent circus in Europe; and in some moods one might think that geniuses of their kind, such as the individual who getting him-self 'airborne' by some apparently haphazard process then balances himself, head downwards, leaning all his weight on one finger on a bottle, may practise their art and bring it to perfection in this quiet and sandy setting. Acrobats, one is often told, rehearse their turns in water, jumping on each other's shoulders, forming human pyramids, and as quickly jumping down, and so forth. Perhaps night club dancers rehearse here on the pale yellow sands. And one must not forget that one of the most insidiously nostalgic of night club tunes, now a circus 'classic' to which performing elephants and seals go through their tricks, the tango *Jalousie*, is of Danish origin. Another name of a night club is the Ritz-Safari, perhaps inspired in daydreams after seeing film versions of Hemingway's 'white hunter' stories. Despite all this, it is only true to say the 'night fever' in Denmark never attains the temperature it did in Roumania where, in towns with a theatrical tradition like Cernauți, one could no longer pretend that anything other than the night club, even the painted churches of Bucovina, were any more of interest, and on arrival meeting the aide-de-camp of the general commanding the district in the hall of the hotel, at breakfast time, we found he had automatically reserved a table for us at the best night club in the evening. The same passion for night life inhabits the Northern Germans in a heavy way, but their touch must ever make it a little sinister or unpleasant, whereas with the Danes it is harmless, whether silly or serious, and on the twelfth stroke of midnight, music and laughing voices die and all is quiet.

This leap-frog progress from town to town now carries us on from Vejle and into Horsens, where Horace Marryat, our friend and travelling companion of a hundred years ago, took up his lodgings at Jørgensens. With less time to spare in a more hurried age we went to Jørgensens for luncheon, and owing to a muddle it took a long, long time. But Jørgensens is an interesting old building with nice exterior, once the house of the Lichtenberg family who were rich merchants of the town. However, its "princely suite in rococo, with stucco ceilings and profiled doors" is a disappointment, and the interior does not live up to the promise of its good façade. It was market day in Horsens. None of those old Jutland peasants "in their picturesque costumes, Hessian boots, velvet breeches, and old cut-coat covered with huge silver buttons"; or the women bringing their rolls of home-made linen to market. But the dress was fast dying out even in Marryat's day. The dining room was full, and by the time luncheon was over, chairs were pulled out and the air was full of cigar smoke. Danes will tell you that a good deal of Jewish blood persists in Vejle and in Horsens. There were, once, many Jewish families in both towns who are by now absorbed into the population, and at Vejle there was a synagogue until 1914. Perhaps this gives market day at Vejle its vitality and energy. Outside the town there is the the Bygholm Castle, now a restaurant, with more 'profiled doors' and stucco ceilings but, in truth, it is not worth the trouble of a visit.

And now another jump on to Skanderborg, the roads being so good that the miles fly past. Here are lakes in most directions and little else, if anything, to look at. It is all fish-

ing, rowing, sailing, and youth hostels and certainly a fine
place for a healthy holiday. And now we are only half an hour
from Aarhus, a great town with more than a hundred thousand
people. It has good modern buildings, better, it seemed to me,
or, at least, seen to more advantage, than in Copenhagen.
There is a large new quarter of museums and zoos and stad-
iums and new university buildings, with a 'nature trail'
winding about for over a mile, "with slips of paper along the
route through which botanists, zoologists, and geologists
make known to visitors their observations on the caprices of
nature. The slips are revised weekly", I quote from the guide
book, but this is where Northern seriousness comes in, for
such a practice could never be possible in the English
climate, though the 'observations' would be worth recording.
Here an entire afternoon was wasted in hysterically funny
circumstances while the kindness and courtesy of various
professors induced them to telephone all over the town for us
in order to find the custodian of the Grauballe man, that
most fascinatingly interesting mummified body found intact
in a bog in Jutland, and apparently the victim of a ritual
sacrifice. Sadly enough, it being a Saturday morning, all their
efforts were in vain. After a *smørrebrød* luncheon which
would have delighted, not so much a pelican, as a spoonbill,
because there were so many delicious objects to be scooped
out of tins, and a misunderstanding at the hotel desk lasting
fifteen minutes because of inability to pronounce Gamle By,*
which means, only and simply, the Old Town museum, we at
last got there. It is a collection of fifty or sixty old houses and
shops, removed bodily, and built into a village, on the same
system as the open air museums outside Stockholm, and at
Oslo and Lillehammer in Norway. But, always, the effect of
such museums is a little 'creepy'. The exhibits are so old and
'horrid'. And if there are not waxwork figures in appropriate
costumes it can only be that it is not the haunted hour. For
those are like the worst nightmare. There are one or two
appalling museums of local costumes in Brittany, and
probably the worst and most frightening of the lot is that

---

* Should English names of Danish origin be pronounced in the
same way, i.e. Whitby, Scalby, Kirkby Moorside?

started by the poet Mistral in his native Provençal town of
Arles. Here at Aarhus all is genuine, and before long one
wishes that some of it was faked. For it is against nature.
There could never be such a collection of old shops and houses,
so close together. The most satisfying results are those at
Williamsburg in Virginia where all is new and rebuilt from
the ground, and it does, undoubtedly, make those recon-
structions more lively if, as at Williamsburg, some objects
are for sale, as for instance, scents and one or two other
trifles in the chemist's shop. At Aarhus it is a dead puppet
show. And at Aarhus there was another mishap, for walking
round the cathedral at one o'clock before luncheon in the
hotel opposite to it, the door into the church was open and it
was reasonable to think it would be open, too, at four or
five o'clock in the afternoon. But not at all. It was herme-
tically closed and the sacristan off duty. In this way I missed
seeing "the interior of the longest cathedral in Northern
Europe", or of "the longest church in Scandinavia", for as
such it is variously described. What is more to the point I
could not see the "intricate baroque monuments of wealthy
burghers and their wives",* and the gilded organ of 1730
which is a favourite with Dr. Schweitzer.

It is north of Aarhus, in the peninsula of Mols that juts out
into the Kattegat, that most of the castles and old manor
houses of Jutland are to be found. But we were to see some of
these a day or two later, and went on due north to Randers.
This is a big town with a few old timber houses, and a town
hall which "once moved three yards on rollers", but no
reason given for it, and one wonders why! And why only three
yards? And again on for another half-hour into Aalborg, much
the pleasantest of the Jutland towns, "to the hotel Phoenix
in the city of Aalborg", which is where Marryat too stayed,
but his visit was over a hundred years ago; and I went into
the Budolfi Church that evening, the dedication being to St.
Botolphus, the English saint and protector of seamen, but
when Marryat saw it, a delightful touch, "old women were

* At the entrance, on the left, lies the chapel of the Marselis family,
with some fine white marble monuments of the seventeenth century
"in the style of Roubilliac" [sic], Horace Marryat.

occupied in cleaning it out, each armed with a goose's wing "
for duster. The interior of this church did seem to be extremely
Northern, as though nearing the end of all things, or *Ultima
Thule*. There is much carving and gilding, nonsensically
pretty, but aggregating little. Then, there is the rococo
doorway of the town hall, more like a private house but for
the *front fuyant* bust of a King above; and the stone built
house of Jens Bang, a rich merchant of the early seventeenth
century, the "biggest and best preserved Renaissance house
in the Scandinavian countries", but what would this be in
Burgos, Siena, or Toledo? It is suitably dour, and built for
a windy climate, and would look well on the main street in
St. Andrews or Aberdeen. Yet there is something quite
delightful about Aalborg. It is so beautifully situated at the
point where the Limfjord widens out and forms a lake, and
there are walks past all the shipping along the waterside.
And for some reason there are gayer restaurants than anywhere else in Denmark excepting Copenhagen, including one
decorated with parrots, and another with paintings of Capri
and the Bay of Naples. Perhaps it is because we are so far
north here that between the beginning of June and the first
of August it is never completely dark at night. And in the
morning we crossed solemnly over the bridge into *Ultima
Thule* in order to have set foot upon North Jutland.

For the land continues for another sixty-four miles. And
what is to seen there? The palace of Dronninglund about
twenty miles from Aalborg, rebuilt by Queen Charlotte
Amalie, widow of Christian V (d. 1699), but with a later
rebuilding, too, after the usual fire, so that it appears there
are no good stucco ceilings. And the dread sounding Skaw,
called, in fact, The Skaw, 'discovered' in the last century by
painters and poets, though little did it avail them, which I
write knowing nothing of their pictures or poems, but feeling,
of instinct, that such discoveries have never helped an artist.
And for the rest? Are the melons of Skagen still famous in
the gastronomic world? Are the peasants of all this district
north of the Limfjord still known as Vendel-boers? Do their
cottages still contain "ship-cabin beds and carved chests of
drawers, painted red and picked out in divers gaudy colours",

as in Hindeloopen and other old towns on the Zuyder Zee? Are there "splendid oleanders, passion flowers, and picotees in the parlour windows"? Marryat has an excellent phrase to describe the meeting of the waters of the Skagerrak and Kattegat; he says "gazing northwards, the land runs tapering finely down like a bullock's tongue". And twelve miles away, out in the middle of the Kattegat, lies the isle of Læsø, beloved of an English gang of encyclopædists; farm houses with thick roots of ribbon seaweed (zostera), a weed which was attacked by disease thirty years ago and is now so rare that the roofs of Læsø are a national curiosity, weed roofs on which grow crops of wild flowers, "yellow stone crop and moon daisy"; and pig farms, and simple inns where the speciality is plaice. Læsø, from the sound of it, is a little on the dull side.

Lovers of Mediterranean shores wandering far afield between the Kattegat and Skagerrak may feel more drawn to Børglum Kloster, a former abbey which came into the hands of Lurids de Thurah of *Den Danske Vitruvius* who restored it, adorning "the Kings' Hall with lifesize portraits of the Oldenburg Kings and Queens of Denmark", putting an altar in the church which takes up the "whole width of the choir, and a stately marble *epitaphium* to the de Thurah family". Børglum Kloster is only some thirty miles from Aalborg, and it was a sad omission not to go there. In such a remote corner of Jutland, even so, that I met no Danes who knew it. Lurids de Thurah had worked and studied in Vienna (as well as Italy) and his Kings' Hall with its Royal portraits is obviously taken from the Kaisersaals in baroque monasteries in Austria. There is, perhaps, even some foreshadowing of the Romantic Movement in it, for it could be that de Thurah had noticed the dynastic affinity of the Habsburg family to the house of Oldenburg, and was making romantic play with this. It is surely a 'romantic' conception to restore an old monastery in the extreme north of Jutland and give to it a little air of Melk upon the Danube and of the Hofburg in Vienna. In a personal and private mythology, therefore, Børglum Kloster is in company with the churches of Lecce and Noto, with the Certosa di Padula, with Taxco and the Santuario de Ocotlán. Even in Jutland it has a touch of those warmer climes, however the winds blow, and it has more music for the spirit than the isle of Læsø.

At the far side of the Limfjord where it swells out into an inland sea, and yields the Limfjord oysters,* is that narrow strip of land with Thisted, capital of the Thy county and, therefore, of Thyland or Thule, whence, if true, came the Varangian bodyguard to keep sentinel by the waters of the Golden Horn. And in the middle of the Limfjord is the island of Mors, with Nykobing, oyster town and Danish caviar centre. Upon a green extremity, or spit of green of this island of Mors, is Feggeklit, where Hamlet was born; and once, long ago, the grave of his brother Fengo was opened and an iron sword taken from it. Smaller and greener still must be the isle of Fuur, where no one goes, but Marryat tells us that the women in his time were remarkable for their marriage head-dress, *a bonnet mirabolant,* as he calls it, "all beads and small feathers like that of a South Sea Islander", and there were gold crowns for the bride. All of which is, of course, long forgotten now.

This is the region of bog burials and *tumuli,* with stories innumerable of the opening of barrows, and of concealed treasures. A boer, crossing a morass, sinks deeper and deeper in the mud, feels something on his leg which he thinks is a snake, and it is a neck ring of solid gold. And there are stories of buried swords which bring ill luck to the finder. It must have supported a large population during the later iron and bronze ages, and that there are still important finds to be made is proved by the recent discoveries of the Egtved woman and the Graubolle man. If, as may well be, there was a thousand or even two thousand years of constant human habitation during those ages, there must be burials beyond number, for the Egtved woman is said to be a thousand years earlier than the Graubolle man. They seem, too, to have been a more interesting people than the Irish bog-dwellers. Innumerable shallow burials, but no conspicuous mounds,

* Said to be the best in Europe, but do they compare with those of Malpeque Bay, in Prince Edward Island, which make our native Whitstables taste of gun-metal?

so that it is hard to know where to begin and research is haphazard; their Kings and Queens, as with the family of Hamlet, being chieftains who slept on heaps of straw, not possessed of the wealth of such petty Kings as those who built the swan-necked Viking ships of Oslo.

Once on the mainland again, and away from the Limfjord, there is the town of Viborg, to which I did not go, having no great expectation of its restored cathedral and fresco paintings by Professor Skovgaard. But now we are in the region, known and seen, round Silkeborg, where there is nothing much except its near-by lakes, and towards Randers. All this is a wonderful holiday country, if you would see nothing except sands and lakes and trees. But we are coming back into the castle district, to names in history, and to the skilled works of human hands. And, first of all, to the minor delights of village churches. For the reader may remember that in front of the Ahlefeldt monument at Odense there was promise of further bewigg'd monuments and effigies to come. This is the place, therefore, to interpolate another and missing example, passed by, when there was opportunity, but, on purpose, in order to gather the rest into one place.

This is the *epitaphium* to Marcus Gjoe (Gøye), d. 1698, in the chapel at Herlufsholm, which is near Sorø, a county town in the middle of Zealand. We passed Sorø every time on the road from Korsør to Copenhagen. The monument is by Th. Quellinus, of a good 'school', as that might be said of dancers or violinists; neat cartouche below, with coat-of-arms of three cockle shells of Santiago; standing female statues, above, between marble pillars, who stand with the air of garden statues; and as background a huge black marble tablet set round with his quarterings and inscribed in Latin. The hero Marcus Gøye reclines on one elbow on a straw palliasse that is too short for him, simulated in white marble, pointing back with the other hand as if at his own achievements. He is in full armour, with magnificently flowing periwig, lace cravat, chains and Orders, the flutings of his armour, the curls of his wig, the bold tying of his sash, all rendered in the marble with a fluid hand. One cupid at his pillow holding a wreath of laurel, and another at his foot carrying a cartouche with his monogram, as that would be worked on linen or upon a seal. His whole figure as good, indeed, as a Roubiliac, and an astonishment to find such an example of the school of Bernini in a village church in Zealand.

But its companion is another monument by Th. Quellinus in a church in Jutland. This is the *epitaphium* to Jørgen Scheel (d. 1695), in Auning church, near Randers. Here, romance and comedy are mingled in confusion. It will be seen that the monument is of a reclining figure lying the other way round from the previous statue, that is to say, leaning on its left elbow, in long curled wig and armour. An angel sounds the last trump beside him while another standing seraph, with a cupid to help her, unfolds a sheet of marble on which the features of a crowned lady appear in bas-relief.

There were, it seems, two Counts Jørgen Scheel, father and son, great landowners, for in their house were tapestries of twelve castles in their possession, and it was said they could ride sixty miles from Grenaa to Viborg on their own land. One of them was Danish Minister to Catherine the Great of Russia, and reputed the handsomest man of his day. He incurred the jealousy of the Empress's favourite, Orloff, and is said to have died poisoned by him.

But the date of this monument is 1695, and the sculptor Th. Quellinus, himself, died in 1709. It cannot, therefore, have been this Count Jørgen Scheel who was Ambassador to the Empress Catherine, and her reputed lover. But it must have been Count Christen Scheel who, we are informed, lived his last three years in St. Petersburg as Danish Envoy to the Russian Court, and died on his post, at only twenty-eight years old, in 1771. On the other hand, the monument to Count Jørgens Scheel by Quellinus does quite clearly show the features of a crowned woman, and she indeed resembles Catherine the Great. All this is mysterious, even though it be true that "Danes wore curled wigs and armour later than other nations", but not as late as 1771, or even fifty years before that. Marryat seems to have said this about the persistence of old fashions in Denmark, suspecting, himself, that the recumbent figure is two generations too early in date to have been the lover of the Russian Empress. One would like to know the correct solution to this puzzle, for the lady of the bas-relief surely *is* the Empress Catherine.*

And, lastly, another *epitaphium*, this time by Fr. Ehbisch, not so good a sculptor as Quellinus, to Geert Diedrich Lewetzau (d. 1737). It is in the church at Tjele, not far from Viborg; a standing marble figure, fully rigged, pistol in hand, with coat-of-arms neatly reposing on a little table, complete with its table cloth, by his side. But in Tjele church there are other Lewetzau monuments, as well, and it was in order to inspect one of these that Horace Marryat got down from his carriage a hundred years ago. "How the winds did blow! Umbrellas turned inside out," etc; "to look at the tomb of a ridiculous puppy of the last century, a certain Capitaine de Lewetzau who left orders in his will that his sarcophagus, all curves and allegory, should be supported by six undraped female figures 'in humble expression of his gratitude to the fair sex for the favours he had received from them in his lifetime'". And the end of the story is that the Lutheran clergyman made a protest, and a compromise was effected by which the ladies were given fishes' tails and became mermaids, and are still there in the church at Tjele holding up the black marble tomb wherein lies the body of the captain.

We had come down all the way from Aalborg in order to see some of the old castles of this part of the country, and were soon driving through twelve miles of woods to Frijsenborg, the huge château of the Krag-Juel-Wind-Frijs family, the greatest landowners of Jutland. This was entirely rebuilt in the middle of last century. When Marryat saw it in 1860, Frijsenborg was to be rebuilt next year. He mentions the Riddersaal, "a magnificent apartment hung with family portraits", but as it now stands Frijsenborg is no less remarkable a monument to that later age, being, indeed, a museum piece of its kind. Few other houses in any land are so complete an epitome of the period 1860 to 1880, giving an extraordinary impression of solid comfort with never shame or remorse in 'pressing the

* The monogrammed initials on cartouches on both this and the previous tomb (at Herlufsholm) are by an expert in lettering, and deserve detailed study.

39   Of Marcus Gøye (*d.* 1698), in the chapel at Herlufsholm

40   Of Jørgen Scheel (*d.* 1695) in Auning Church

Both by Th. Quellinus

EPITAPHIA

41   LISELUND: The "Cottage Orné"

42   A street of eighteenth-century houses in Tønder

bell'; there must have been such hosts of servants ready and waiting. Everything is perfect at Frijsenborg down to the smallest detail, and I do not think the answer is that it is all ugly. The age was sure of itself, and security and optimism are so lacking as qualities in our day that it is a solace to the nerves to feel the breath of their ghosts upon us. Only one wing of the house is now lived in, and awake in the middle of the night one could but envy them their carriaged lives.

Having stayed up late talking to our host we only started next morning in time to go out for luncheon. But our destination could stand as model for the the smaller Danish manor house. It lay near the Randers Fjord at a village, I think, called Tved. The house consisted of a small central body of one floor, with wings to either side. In one of the wings lived the octogenarian father of the owner, an old gentleman gone into the town of Randers for some local festivity, and due home again next day. Such a building is a lesson in how to give distinction by the simplest means. It is so evidently the house of a country gentleman, with its Riddersaal and portraits of the house of Oldenburg, the Kings with *le front fuyant* much in evidence and the Queens in great crinolines. All round are farm buildings and bucolic air. A small country house of this size and scale in England would have taken the form of a simple cube or block, as in some red brick rectory or old square of stone. It would never have been planned, in simplicity, on so grand a layout, with *cour d'honneur*, side wings, and *Riddersaal*, and one is inclined to believe this must be the influence and example of the Absolute Kings of this small kingdom. Only to judge by the Royal portraits in so many of the old houses the Danes had their monarchical system much in mind, for in no other country do you see so many likenesses of kings and queens. In no part of Denmark, we were told, more than here in Jutland. The whole family had lived in England, and loved to talk of London. With its fine pieces of old furniture it was as delightful a country house as one could wish to see.

We had now to cross the Randers Fjord in order to approach the big tract of country between Randers and Grenaa, where there is so much to see. Auning church lies out

in the middle of this, with its Roubiliac-like monument to
Count Jørgen Scheel and *sudario*-like portrait of a crowned
Empress displayed behind him. Only a few miles away is the
round church of Thorsager, which I could not visit, of the
significantly pagan name, the unique example of its sort in
Jutland, standing on a hill, we were told, so that it towers
above the village; but it has been much restored and has, in
any case, not the flavour of the round churches in the isle of
Bornholm. But the interest of this projecting part of Jutland
is its old castles, in which it is as rich as Funen. And there are
the two towns, Grenaa with a few half-timbered houses of
the eighteenth century, and Ebeltoft down at its southern
extremity, not much bigger than a village, with cobbled
streets and houses of half-timber. This may have a pretty,
magpie character.

Instead, we went to Rosenholm. This is a castle of immortal
and imperishable poetry, even though not of exceptional
content in any particularity. That is to say, to an Englishman
it is the home of the Rosenkrantzs which, alone, and by itself,
means a great deal.* And without containing any works of
art of a higher order it has most of those things which a castle
of its name and history should have, in the way of portraits,
tapestries, and furniture. There is a wonderful array of
sixteenth century portraits, starting from Jørgens Rosenkrantz who built Rosenholm, and with Holger Rosenkrantz,
a learned member of the family who built two schools and
taught in them, himself. But what a name is Rosenkrantz
(Crown of Roses)! And in Jutland, especially, where the
noblest names are of plebeian meaning, as Høg, portending
falcon, and therefore better than it sounds, Krag, Krabbe,
and Bille. The origin of the name Rosenkrantz, which is
probably legendary, being that one of the family went with
an early king on pilgrimage to Rome and was given by the
Pope a golden rose, at the same time that the Pope gave a
golden violet to the King. But, at least, in the words of
Marryat, the name of Rosenkrantz "is of great antiquity; all

* I enquired in Denmark, as many Englishmen would do, of the
family of Gyldenstjerne, and was told they are now extinct in Denmark but still living in Sweden.

you hear of that blood is good, illustrious, and well spoken of in the annals of the country"; and he goes on to tell us, which is more interesting, that the Jutland peasants will point out, around the manor of Herringsholm, which is said to have been in the possession of their family since the sixteenth century, numerous barrows, where the earlier members of the family lie interred.* Lost, in truth, 'in the mists of antiquity'; but with this difference between the Rosenkrantzs and old Irish families like that of the O'Conor Don, Prince of Toolavin, or MacGillycuddy of the Reeks, that the Rosen-krantzs have filled positions of political importance until recent times, till, indeed, they opposed the assuming of absolute Kingship when they suffered exile and their estates were confiscated.

Here, at Rosenholm, are portraits of Erik Rosenkrantz, Ambassador to the Protector, who, when Cromwell mocked him for his youthful appearance because he had no beard, replied: "If my sovereign had known it was a beard you re-quired, he could have sent you a goat; at any rate, my beard is of older date than your Protectorate." And the Protectorate soon ended; so, for that matter, did beards, for the periwig came in and beards were out of fashion for two hundred years and more. So Erik preserved his dignity; and Marryat tells us, in a footnote, that the engraved frontispiece to his funeral sermon represents his *epitaphium*, in which an angel is pictured as descending from heaven and placing a crown of roses on his brow. But at Rosenholm he is painted with his three wives, all wearing the same pattern of white satin gown. We were shown over Rosenholm by Baroness Rosenkrantz and her brother-in-law Baron Arild; and it is evident that in Denmark the sort of fame and legend attach to Rosenholm that centre in England round Warwick Castle. It is accepted, that is to say, as part of the history of the country. That it is still inhabited by the family, is, as always, an immeasurable enhancement of its qualities.

The church of Hornslet, only a short distance away, is

---

* At Ledreborg in Zealand an old barrow or tumulus now holds the family tombs. This sounds like a conscious Gothicism making addition to an old legend.

hardly less romantic, for it contains the tombs of the Rosen-krantzs. Here is another Erik Rosenkrantz, who had custody of Bothwell, and brought him prisoner from Norway. It is hardly an exaggeration to say that you feel in this chapel at Hornslet as near to the immortal presence of Shakespeare, himself, as in front of his own tomb in the church at Stratford-on-Avon. For here on so many *epitaphia* are the engraved alliances of Rosenkrantz and Gyldenstjerne with all their coats-of-arms. It is said that between eighty and a hundred of the blood of Rosenkrantz lie buried here. The effigies are not particularly remarkable; the poetry lies in the sound and association of their names. As such, it must ever be imperishable, for to have your name mentioned by Shakespeare is to enjoy immortal fame. To have been friends and companions of Hamlet, Prince of Denmark, is romance indeed. And it was an experience to be shown the family tombs by the son of the house, in person.

Rosenholm is not the end of the castles of East Jutland. Among several more are Sostrup standing in its moat, and Rugård which lies in a wood upon a lake not far from the seashore. And there is Gammel Estrup, now turned into Jutland's Manor Museum, and surely more beautiful when Marryat saw it, still in the hands of the Scheel family who owned it, and are buried in the church at Auning. He drove, as usual, through the gård and gateway, "crossing two separate moats of bright sparkling running water from the Randers Fjord, swans in numbers and cygnets, too, the heraldic bearings of the house of Scheel", and descended in the inner court of the castle to be received by the Count's brother-in-law, "Captain Sparling of the Hussars". They walked through the garden; "in green *caisses* stood gigantic orange-trees in full blossom and perfume, nearly coeval with the building" which dates from the early sixteenth century. He tells of a saal "entirely hung round with oval portraits, many of them very charming, by Jens Juel"; long corridors hung with portraits, and black wood brass-bound chests along the passages, "old beds of needlework, old mirrors, powder and pomade boxes, tables covered with old Dutch tiles", this last, a Danish custom seen nowhere else. Now, at

Gammel Estrup, there is admission all the year round, and it is one of many old houses and castles which we may feel certain were more beautiful still when there was no admission at all and no notices, "1 Kr., children 50 øre. In summer 60 øre, and 30 øre", respectively.

One of the main inducements in coming to Jutland had been in order to see Clausholm. It was, therefore, most fitting that this culmination should have came upon the afternoon of our last day in Denmark, for it more than fulfilled all expectation. Clausholm has to an extraordinary degree an air of melancholy and departed grandeur. Marryat, who is the very touchstone of old Denmark, remarks of Frederik IV that "he never saw his plasterwork surpassed in any country, and that in all his buildings you have richly moulded ceilings to perfection". This had been the first inspiration to seeing Clausholm, for it was thence that the King had eloped with his Reventlow 'conscience Queen'. And she was born and died at Clausholm. But this was not the King's only 'conscience' escapade. Some years before, while his queen, Louisa of Mecklenburgh, was still alive, he fell in love with the daughter of the Prussian Minister Viereck. In the presence of her father, the Cabinet Ministers, and the Councillors of State, he wedded her and created her Countess of Antvorskov. She died in childbirth during the next year.* Her father, writing to Count Wartenberg, in explanation of this curious alliance, an account of which had to be submitted to the King of Prussia, writes, "the marriage has been consummated in presence of the Ministers and Councillors. He hopes the King will not have *mauvais sentiments* on the subject; he has consulted the Bible, and he does not find a single word by which a King and Sovereign Prince is forbidden to have more than one wife—it is only the obstinacy of the Church." Luther and Melancthon, he had been interested to discover, had permitted an Elector of Hesse to have two wives. "As disgraceful a

---

* She is buried in the church of St. Saviour's at Copenhagen, the church with the elephant organ-case and all the cupids playing at the font. During his youth "the King had entertained a deep passion for an Italian lady of high family, a Countess Velo, and would have married her, but she was of the Catholic persuasion."

history as ever occurred in the annals of any civilized country", that is some historians' view of it; or was it only that Frederik IV was both a little after, and before, his day?

Like the palace of the Sleeping Beauty, Clausholm is lost in the high woods. And when at last you get there, the arms of the Reventlow Queen are still painted on the great wooden doors of the gateway, with her crown. This has the touch of Italy, perhaps painted by some itinerant Italian of the theatre. And coming through the gateway you turn to the left into the court of Clausholm. The building is tall and gaunt, of no ornament but a periwigg'd bust above the doorway, which could be a portrait of the King, or of the Grand Chancellor Reventlow, father of the 'conscience Queen'. The stucco ceilings at Clausholm are the most splendid imaginable, but dating, curiously, not from the years the Queen was banished here, but from 1690–1700 in the lifetime of her father the Grand Chancellor. There are ceilings by the same stuccoists at Fredensborg, and the only work at all approaching it in fantasy and richness is to be found in some of the old houses at The Hague which are by the architect Daniel Marot, who was a Huguenot. They are in the same late Louis XIV style though, in fact, nothing of the kind is to be seen in France. One would almost assume on the strength of this, that the Clausholm ceilings are by the the same hands, but they are the work of stuccoists from the Swiss canton of the Tessin or Ticino, and in particular the brothers Carbonetti and Francesco Quadri.* Perhaps, therefore, the ceilings at The Hague are by sculptors from the Ticino, which would

---

* "Quelques eclaircissements sur des stucateurs tessinois en Danemark au XVIII Siecle", an article by B L. Grandjean in *Zeitschrift fur Schweizerische Archaologie and Kunstgeschichte*, Band 15, 1954, Heft 2, Verlag Birkhauser, Basle, pp. 99–102. The first sentences read: "Il est bien connu qu'aucune autre contrée de l'Europe a certainement vue naître autant de stucateurs fameux que le canton du Tessin. Anx XVII et XVIII Siècles ils sont partis des petits villages aux bords des lacs et dans les montagnes vertes, et presque partout en Europe on trouve les traces de leur art merveilleux et leur technique supérieure." This explains the emergence of so great an artist as Franz Anton Bustelli, the modeller of Nympenburg porcelain figures, who came from near Lugano, in the Ticino.

solve that mystery. Room after room is to be admired at Clausholm, inexhaustible in fantasy, with fabulous animals, *putti*, antique heads, little landscapes, sphinxes and cornucopias. The fertility of invention is astonishing. On the two floors there must be some fifteen rooms with stucco ceilings, some few of them touched with gold, but mostly in snow-white stucco with, now one knows their secret, some suggestion of the steep snows. It is an amazing revelation in this remote house in Denmark to find work of this quality all done, it is evident, in a short space of time, the Swiss sculptors perhaps spending the summer months at Clausholm over a few years, after which the spell was cast upon the palace. The 'conscience Queen' came back to live here for twelve years, disgraced and banished by her husband's son and successor, Christian VI, and died in one of these rooms in 1743. Since then, it is as though nothing has happened in the palace, and for its melancholy beauty Clausholm is unforgettable and unique. It is perhaps scarcely to be credited that such poetry could be conferred upon an old house by its stucco ceilings. Yet, when they are of this degree of excellence it is more in the aggregate than coming to Clausholm in order to see one painting. That would have to be of an incomparable rarity that it should in itself become part of its surroundings and not convey the message that it would be seen equally well in a museum. But the ceilings here are superlative and quite exceptional, and they speak of the old splendour in this sleeping palace. Marryat, who was alive to the beauty of it, says it would be pleasant to dream of Clausholm and this is, indeed, its quality. Even its upper rooms that are empty of furniture are a part of the beauty of Denmark.

So potent is the flavour of this old house that it was summer when we entered it, and autumn when we came out. It was a September evening as we drove through the long woods to Frijsenborg. And next morning in the falling rain we took the road for home. But on the way, or rather, a little out of the way, we were to stop at Christiansfeld, which is a Moravian settlement. It is a village of a few hundred inhabitants, laid out on a regular plan, with many of the square houses of the Moravians still standing. They are dwindled in numbers, and unfortunately no longer wear their sober, distinctive dress; young girls in deep red, unmarried women pink; married blue; and widows grey or white. But the honey cakes of Christiansfeld are still on sale, though not nearly as good as Danish almond cakes. The chapel of the Moravians has a quiet beauty of its own, it is so high and square and empty, with its wooden floor and scrubbed wooden benches, devoid of any form of ornament. The hotel with the good long name, Brødremenighedens Hotel hos Stricker, is the property of the Brethren, with old bits of furniture and engravings, and serving Cutlet à la Moravien, which may be the *escallope de veau* "cut like a *tournedos* and dressed with a *purée* of cod's roe, red herring and shredded horseradish", 'fed to' to recent travellers from England*. Their meal ended with asparagus tips drenched with brandy, followed by liqueurs served with pancakes stuffed with blackcurrant jam and mounted with whipped cream. After which, as they say, "the black coffee was both welcome and very fine". But on the day of our call at Christiansfeld the hotel had been invaded by a barbarian horde out of a char-a-banc, and it was pleasant to take refuge from them in the Moravian cemetery. This, like their simple chapel, has a quality that touches the heart. It is a simplicity of 1773, kept unaltered, but now losing its hold, the Moravians being concerned more with missionary work and having shed most of those peculiarities that made them like living primitives in a world that they could keep at a safe distance and control. Little is left, now, except the etching of their chapel, which keeps a breath of that simple poetry, upon a glass ash-tray. The rest is fading, and in a few years will be gone.

Now it only remains to turn back as far as Kolding, and take the road across the neck of Jutland back to Esbjerg, seeing little on the way but pleasant country and one old manor house set back from the road, with formal layout reminiscent of the old house at Tved. In an hour and a half we were in Esbjerg among the week-old English newspapers, waiting for the hour of embarkation. And after a horribly

* *Holiday in Denmark with Bon Viveur*, London, Frederick Muller Ltd., 1955, pp. 80, 81.

rough summer crossing, and a last *smørrebrød* luncheon, back again at Harwich, which is the beginning and the end of going to Denmark for a holiday.

It is possible, however, to prolong that for a day or two by making a hypothetical journey to a near corner of Denmark. This is the part lying between Esbjerg and the frontier with Germany, and it will be recalled that we have already been to Ribe. We will spend a few hours in the region below that, and our account of it need take no longer in the reading than as many minutes. First and foremost, it is to visit Tønder. We saw a poster of its red brick houses in the red brick square of Ribe, and formed an immediate conclusion that it must have a small and very special character of its own. This seems to be borne out in all accounts of Tønder, which is but an hour from Ribe. Or, now, back in England, is Tønder better in the imagination than in fact? In the poster it looked like Williamsburg in Virginia, but on a more modest scale. The beauty of Williamsburg being that it is ridiculous, and quite new, though genuine. There are certain red brick houses in England, notably Chichele, in Buckinghamshire, which have this particular red brick quality. It is something that, curiously, you do not find in Holland, where you would expect it, though in humble guise it is present in the little streets of houses built for the Dutch colony at Potsdam. There, it has association with the giant Prussian grenadiers who may have lodged in these little brick houses, and had to lower their heads because of their high, half-mitre or sugar-loaf caps as they came in at the door. But that is all fantasy because, of course, they lived in barracks. Nevertheless, one has in mind that there must be, somewhere, an Arcadia of red brick buildings. In the Close at Salisbury it may seem near at hand. One looks for it, in vain, among the Moravians; and there is the hint of it in Mennonite farms in Lincoln County, Pennsylvania, among the Old and New Orders of Amish, and the Dunkers. I thought, at one time, that the Cloister of Ephrata was the answer. This was a society for the Solitary, built along the silent waters of Cocalico Creek. It was founded by Johann Conrad Beissel who came to America in 1719. The men wore the dress of white friars, a

153

long white robe reaching to the heels, a sash or girdle round the waist, and a cowl hanging down the neck. They printed Bunyan's *Pilgrim's Progress*, translated into their own primitive dialect of German. But, unfortunately, the Cloister of Ephrata proves to be a three-storeyed wooden building. Later, it seemed as though it could be in Friesland, in the Town Halls at Sneek and Dokkum. But this, too, was a delusion, despite their green council rooms painted with *chinoiseries* and the rows of long clay pipes put out for the town councillors to smoke. But, after all, it does exist and is to be found at Tønder.

It would be better, however, to approach it not through Ribe but by way of the island of Als, which is as though we had continued straight down south from Christiansfeld. Als is indeed, hardly an island, for it is only a few hundred feet from the mainland, but it has the dynastic towns of Sønderborg and Augustenborg. At Sønderborg we miss the parish church where Marryat saw "some of the most extraordinary specimens of carved and gilt *epitaphia*", in one of which he counted as many as twelve or fourteen different portraits, "each held suspended from the hands of a golden angel". And in the palace chapel the coffins were opened for him and he saw the withered mummy of a "young girl of twenty-two, attired in a black velvet dress and point lace, her fair flaxen hair hanging loosely down, and hands crossed meekly on her bosom". At Augustenborg, a much smaller place, there is another palace once the home of that dynasty with sloping foreheads and now, unkindly, an asylum, which is a pity because there is splendid plasterwork in some of the rooms. This is by a Swiss-Italian sculptor from the Ticino of a later generation than those who worked at Clausholm,* stucco work of curious character, for it includes rococo

---

* See footnote to page 150. The sculptor was M. A. Taddei (1755–1831). He arrived in Sleswig in 1777, and carved bas-reliefs, ceilings, and overdoors for Baron Geltingen in the manor house of the same name. In the same year he began work in the palace of Augustenborg, returning to his native canton in 1786. He does not seem to have worked outside Sleswig–Holstein, or nearer to Denmark proper than the isle of Als.

ornaments, pots of flowers, landscapes, and large framed wall-scenes in the antique taste such as *Hannibal at Capua*, with lifesize Roman figures seated at a table. There can be little or nothing else at either Augustenborg or Sønderborg; and now it is a matter of forty miles to Tønder. But all the way it is but a mile or two from the German frontier and this should be borne in mind, for certainly the character of Tønder is affected by it.

Tønder, when we get there, is a little town with only seven thousand inhabitants. We are only a few miles from the North Sea coast and approaching the sandy Frisian islands, in sign of which is the speciality of asparagus soup given at one of the hotels in Tønder, as asparagus grows best in sandy soils. It should lie, therefore, in the midst of marshes, and this it does for of old there were terrible floods and inundations, and now the sea waters are only held back by a huge dyke system. In one night in 1634 more than fifty thousand domestic animals, and as many human beings as there are people living in Tønder, were all drowned in the fens between Ribe and Tønder. It is a fen or marshland town, though surrounded by grasslands and cornfields, and should have the special character of such towns. One wonders if it will at all resemble towns like Wisbech with a canalized river in the middle and fine old houses on both banks! Or those fenland villages, Terrington St. Clement, Wiggenhall St. Mary Magdalen, 'the Walpoles', Walsoken, and West Walton, all with fine stone churches, the stone having been carried by barge, all in the marshlands? Or that other line of churches, Long Sutton, Gedney, Holbeach, Whaplode, Moulton, and Weston, all in a line of fifteen miles over the fens between Long Sutton and Spalding! But, of course, Tønder is not at all like these, being a little town in a remote part of Denmark, so near to Germany that it has passed more than once into German hands.

There is an old church at Tønder, but it cannot in any way resemble the English fenland churches which are always influenced by the proximity of magnificent and enormous abbeys and churches such as Ely. Everything in Denmark is upon a more miniature scale. There are none of our towering monuments like Durham, or Salisbury, or Lincoln. The church at Tønder is rich in woodcarvings of the local Sleswig style. It has a carved and painted reredos in three storeys reaching to the ceiling, a wooden gallery and organ loft. But the character of Tønder comes from its two sorts of houses. The best account of the town, and indeed the only one worth reading, mentions the strong Germanic influence in the gables and pediments, and the beautiful doorways in two streets, the Østergade and Westergade, often with stone animals to guard the door. There are, this says, "private houses with the most beautiful old bay windows, some with painted doors as richly decorative as the furniture of Tyrol". These are the houses of merchants, tradesmen, town councillors, and burghers.

The other sort of house was lived in by the lacemakers. For Tønder had a local industry in lace, at its most flourishing in the eighteenth century. The Tønder lace is still famous. The cottages of the lace makers are at the back of the bigger houses. This is what the aforementioned writers have to say of them: "One street in particular, the Ulgade, curves with an S-bend. The little stone treads, rectangular and very neatly whitened, face each front door. Every door and every set of house windows is painted a different colour, and beside each set of steps a rose tree is growing. We saw these straight little round-topped trees when the roses were in full bloom. The tiled roofs glowed like ripe apricots on a south wall and the long pointed shadows lay on the cobblestones."

Only five kilometres away there is the little village of Møgeltønder, with the castle of Schackenborg outside it, a large baroque building with more plasterwork by one of the brothers Taddei, from far Ticino. But Møgeltønder is like a little edition of Tønder, with the Slotsgade, a street of old houses that have thatched roofs and a lime avenue, as well. It is apparent that Tønder and Møgeltønder must be two of the prettiest places in the Kingdom of Denmark. They are idyllic in their little line of architecture which connects onto such widely different places as Kitzbühel and Dinkelsbühl, or towns such as Lübeck and Bremen and Hamburg, before the great fire of 1842. Though Danish, this is part of the Dutch and German influence, and of town or village architecture in a line from Strasbourg in Alsace to Cracow in Poland, and thence to Danzig.

This is a corpus of building, the body of which has never been gathered into one book. And in its own small way it has lines of communication that join it to the villages of Dutch Friesland, which is not far away. Only, indeed, across the opening of the Elbe. Several place names in this part of Southern Jutland, such as Husum, Løgum, Ballum, have the typical Frisian termination in the syllable 'um' as Dokkum, Marsum, Makkum, Workum, Kollum, Hallum, in Dutch Friesland. The population of all the Frisian islands is of Frisian origin as far as the isles of Föhr and Sylt, which isles were Danish until the war of 1863 when Denmark lost Sleswig to Germany. There is an unbroken chain of these names on the mainland, running parallel to the curve of the Frisian Islands, Oldersum, Pewsum, Lottersum, across the Emsand in Germany, continuing with Amrum, Keitum, Morsum, which are on the German isle of Sylt.

For now we reach the Frisian Islands that are still Danish. Rømø, the first of these, had been seized by the Germans after the war of 1863 and was only returned to Denmark in 1920. But they are of more than passing interest to Englishmen, for it is along these coasts, in Friesland, in the islands, and in Jutland, that is found the nearest foreign equivalent to English as a spoken language. There are parts of Jutland, as there are of Friesland, where a person speaking broad Yorkshire would feel quite at home. And not Yorkshire, only, Northumbrian, too; and indeed this may be true of most of our East coast inflection, for are not the fishwives of Leith, who are to be seen in their striped dresses hawking fish in the streets of Edinburgh, said to be of Jutish origin? They are decidedly, of Jutish or Frisian appearance. It is a physical type still to be met with in the Yorkshire dales, and denoting a Danish or a Jutish ancestry, though we shall see, shortly, that there are contradictions in this. And at the same time that we mention the absence of any study of all that complex body of building of which Tønder and Møgeltønder are a

157

little part, it could be suggested that another study of fascinating interest would be the fishing population of all the coasts of Europe from Norway to Portugal, a thesis which would bring out some curious puzzles. In every instance it will be the primitive population that stays on the coast and continues to go fishing. And with the original Frisians the distinctive feature is their excessively fair hair.

Rømø is no distance at all from Tønder, except that in these flat landscapes, as in Holland, their own special laws of relativity seem to be in force. Four or five miles from Tønder to the North Sea Coast, and then about a dozen miles along the dunes to the causeway. And what is there to see when you are in Rømø, which is one of the ends of the world to those not born and reared there? The interest is that Rømø had prosperity as a whaling port. Their men-folk sailed far away from Rømø to Iceland and Greenland, and after a year or more's absence returned, rich men. This was during the eighteenth century. And there are, as well, some big old farms. There is the Kommandorgaarden, an 'ancestral farm' of this period, with the original painted walls and ceiling, now restored and made into a regional farm museum, a temple of Ceres in sight of the biggest stretch of dunes in Denmark. In the churchyard are tombstones of the 'Commanders', that is to say, whaling captains of the eighteenth century, and in the interior of the church the distinguishing factor would seem to be the hat pegs of wrought iron in position above every pew. There are only 750 inhabitants in all Rømø; an island to dream of, alike when you are too hot in the tropics, or if whaling near Bear Island or Spitzbergen and Rømø is your warm home. It must have been a most curious community of old, with the men-folk pitching and tossing hundreds of miles away, and the women and children going no further than Skærbek or their metropolis Ribe upon market day.

Lastly, we come north again through Ribe and right into Esbjerg, for that is the only way to get to Fanø. It is only twenty minutes from Esbjerg in the ferry to that little and secluded world of its own, now, of course, a holiday centre because of its sandy beaches, but with bad or indifferent hotels. It is, also, the only place in Denmark where local costume is still worn. The dress is black, but much embroidered. Formerly, a multitude of coloured petticoats was worn, as with the fisherfolk of Scheveningen on the Zuyder Zee. Marryat, crossing on the boat from Esbjerg a hundred years ago, made a study of one of the "fair inhabitants", and very fair, he says, they were; a young maiden "leaning over the cargo talking away to the watermen", and he with difficulty counted: a green woollen petticoat bound with black velvet, a blue, then red, followed by brown, then yellow, and a second blue, making, in all, a round number of six, but there are stories of an absolute maximum of thirteen. He continues, "but the oddest custom of all is that of wearing a black mask, similar to those worn at the *bal masqué*—minus the *bavolet*, when working out in the fields . . . Anything more ludicrous cannot be imagined than a troop of these black-masked creatures returning home, driving their cows from the downs. It seems to affect the ewes, too, for we met several new born lambs, white as the driven snow, with black masks exactly like their mistresses. The children are very handsome, and the girls at the cottage windows prettier than anything we have come across for many a day. They have quite an Oriental type of countenance—long eyes, dark, *fendu à l'amande*, aquiline nose, fine and delicate mouth, a dark but brilliant complexion; even the fashion of the masks (though our grandmothers of the eighteenth century never walked or rode out without wearing these *loups*, as they were then termed) gives the impression as if they were some remnant of customs imported from an Eastern land; and what with the Varangians and early connexion with Turkey, it is not at all impossible that it may be so."

No excuse is offered for making this long quotation, for it is the best account of Fanø. The masks or gags were to keep off the flying sand; but they became the fashion and more than one early Queen of Denmark was painted wearing it. But the mask, as now worn, is a more simple affair consisting only of a scarf round the neck which can be pulled up to protect the face and eyes.* One of the most interesting points in Marryat's

* Worn also by the islanders of Læsø, out in the Kattegat. What greater contrast could be imagined than between these black-masked

description is his inference that some, at least, of the inhabitants were of dark complexion. But this is one of the mysteries, too, of some of the Dutch islands, ascribed, locally, to contact with the Spanish soldiers in the time of Alva. It would seem more probable that there are two basic types of primitive inhabitant, one dark, and the other and later influx very fair; the dark being of that dark Celtic type which is to be seen in Ireland, and also in the typical Scots Highlander. Marryat's theory of contact with Turkey is, needless to say, absurd. Wherever the Varangian bodyguard came from, it is highly improbable that they ever returned to their distant home bringing with them Greek brides.

If Rømø is, or was, a whaling port, then Fanø is a seal island. This gives, always, a shock or impact of the north. Who, that has ever seen it, forgets the shop in the main street of Tromsø, in the north of Norway, which is hung from ceiling to floor with huge polar bear skins! And even the sealskins of Fanø give a little of that same sensation. It is the touch of the Arctic, there being no town anywhere far enough south in the world to give an Antarctic or Antipodean feeling, unless it be some fog and storm-bound fishing village in Tierra del Fuego. So Fanø is northern; and it may seem more northern than any other place in Denmark excepting The Skaw, on its spit of land between the Skagerrak and Kattegat. The black costume of Fanø is entirely northern, yet such as might be worn with jet ornaments in fishing villages on the Yorkshire coast, but notably at Flamborough Head, where the headland within the Flamborough Dyke is sometimes known as "Little Denmark".

But there is confusion in Yorkshire between Anglian, Danish, and Norwegian names. There were separate invasions of England by Northmen from Norway, and by Danes from Jutland, though Yorkshire place names ending in "by", of which there are nineteen instances, must certainly have been brought by Danes. It would be reasonable to assume that the Northmen from Norway went to Northumbria, and the Danes to Yorkshire. The mouth of the Humber was "like an open gate

Jutlanders, and the 'veiled men' or Touaregs of the Sahara. But the reason for it, in both cases, is the same! It is the flying sand.

to the Danes", says one authority; and eventually the Dane-law comprised all that part of England lying east of the Watling Street, from Chester to London. But they settled in Lincolnshire even more than Yorkshire. One hundred and ninety-five places in Lincolnshire, a third of the whole number, end in the characteristic Danish "by", and seventy-six more in "thorpe". Lincolnshire is, therefore, pre-eminently the Danish part of England, and it is just opposite this stretch of coast. Climatically it must be the same.

One of the strains in our English blood, undiluted, is to be seen along these shores. And what shores! On one side of Fanø it is possible to drive twelve miles in a straight line along the sands. The village of Sønderho in the south of Fano has old sealers' cottages, and ship models hanging in the church. The houses are of one storey, and the thatch as close as mouse-fur. The women of Fanø in their black dresses are waiting to be photographed. In an hour the boat leaves Esbjerg, and there will be nothing left but memories of Denmark. It seems a long way from Fanø to the Amalienborg, to the treasures of Rosenborg, and to Italian pantomimes, nightly, in the Tivoli Gardens. We are at one side of Denmark, and those are at the other, one hundred and seventy miles away. Yet, within this small space is an old kingdom and a race apart, not to be confused with either the Norwegians or the Swedes. The impressions one carries away, besides those memories already named, will be of lakes and beechwoods, of, it may be, Clausholm, Vallø, and the Valdemar Slot; little in scale, and minor, but not melancholy in key. But, above all, of a people who are neither rich, nor poor, who have solved many of the problems of living in this twentieth century, and are without the anxieties of the French, the contrasts of Italy, or the agonies of Spain. It is this which is the lesson of Denmark. It is a small country, but things are in their proper proportion. There is enough of the old to form a tradition, and enough of the new to form a style. And the boat lifts anchor, and flat fertile Denmark fades back into the sky.

13 July—9 August 1955.

Index

The numbers in **heavy type** refer to the *figure numbers* of the illustrations.